Jewish
Reflections
on
Death

JEWISH

REFLECTIONS

ON

DEATH

Edited by Jack Riemer

Foreword by Elisabeth Kubler-Ross

SCHOCKEN BOOKS · NEW YORK

First SCHOCKEN PAPERBACK edition 1976

7 6 5 4 3   79 80 81 82

Copyright © 1974 by Schocken Books Inc.
Manufactured in the United States of America

Library of Congress Cataloging in Publication Data

Riemer, Jack, comp.
  Jewish reflections on death.

  1. Death (Judaism) I. Title.
BM635.4.R53 1975   296.3'3   74-18242

dedicated to

those who have gone before us
   who showed us the way,

to those who travel with us
   who brighten the way,

and to those who will come after us
   who we pray will continue the way

and to the people of Beth Abraham Synagogue
   whom I have taught and from whom I have learned.

ACKNOWLEDGMENTS

Rabbi Chaim R. Denburg for selections from *Code of Jewish Law: Yoreh Deah* translated by Chaim N. Denburg, published by Jurisprudence Press, Montreal, Canada. Copyright 1954 by Chaim N. Denburg.

The Jewish Spectator for the translation of *Histalkut Hanefesh* by Samuel H. Dresner, which originally appeared under the title "The Art of Dying," February, 1958; and for "Death in Jerusalem" by Jacob Neusner, November, 1973. Both copyright by *The Jewish Spectator*.

Elie Wiesel for "The Death of My Father," from *Legends of Our Time,* published by Holt, Rinehart & Winston. Copyright 1968 by Elie Wiesel.

Commentary Magazine and Hans J. Morgenthau for "Death in the Nuclear Age." Reprinted from *Commentary*, by permission. Copyright © 1961 by the American Jewish Committee.

Farrar, Straus & Giroux, Inc. and Sylvia Heschel for "Death as Homecoming," originally published as "Reflections on Death." Reprinted with the permission of Farrar, Straus & Giroux, Inc. "Reflections on Death" was first published in *Conservative Judaism.* The essay is by the late Abraham Joshua Heschel, copyright © 1973 by Sylvia Heschel, executrix of the Estate of Abraham Joshua Heschel.

The Jewish Advocate for "The Halakhah of the First Day" by Joseph B. Soloveitchik, which was the first part of a lecture-tribute given on the Shloshim Memorial Observance for Rabbi M. Z. Twersky. Copyright © 1972 by *The Jewish Advocate.*

Judaism: A Quarterly Journal for permission to reprint "Death as Estrangement" by Emanuel Feldman. Reprinted from *Judaism: A Quarterly Journal*, Winter 1972, pages 59–66. *Judaism* is published by the American Jewish Congress.

The Viking Press, Inc. for permission to reprint the letter by Henrietta Szold. From *Henrietta Szold: Life and Letters* edited by Marvin Lowenthal. Copyright 1942 by The Viking Press, Inc. Copyright © renewed 1970 by Herman C. Emer and Harry L. Shapiro, executors for the Estate of Marvin Lowenthal. Reprinted by permission of The Viking Press, Inc.

The Jewish Frontier Publishing Association for permission to reprint "The Right to Kill," from Volume I of *The Inner Eye* by Hayim Greenberg. Copyright 1953 by the Jewish Frontier Publishing Association. And "Conversation with a Dying Man," which originally appeared under the title "On Death," from Volume II of *The Inner Eye* by Hayim Greenberg. Copyright 1964 by the Jewish Frontier Publishing Association.

Abraham Kaplan for "Life and Death as Partners," based upon "On Death" in *Love and Death* by Abraham Kaplan, published by the University of Michigan Press, Ann Arbor, Michigan. Copyright 1973 by Abraham Kaplan.

Harcourt, Brace, Jovanovich, Inc. for "To Hold with Open Arms." From *A Believing Jew* by Milton Steinberg, copyright, 1951, by Edith Steinberg. Reprinted by permission of Harcourt, Brace, Jovanovich, Inc.

Union of American Hebrew Congregations for "Death Be Proud" by Michael Braude. Reprinted from *Brotherhood Magazine*, January – February, 1972. Copyright 1972 by the Union of American Hebrew Congregations.

Max Lerner for "My Father 'Moved' " by Max Lerner, copyright by Max Lerner, 1951.

Rabbi Leo Jung for "The Meaning of the Kaddish" by Leo Jung, published by the Union of Orthodox Jewish Congregations under the title "The Kaddish at the Grave." Copyright 1926 by Leo Jung.

Mrs. Goldye Adler, executrix of the Estate of Rabbi Morris Adler, for "We Do Not Stand Alone" by Morris Adler.

B'nai B'rith *National Jewish Monthly* and Rabbi Eugene J. Lipman for "The Minyan Is a Community" by Eugene J. Lipman. Copyright 1971 by the B'nai B'rith *National Jewish Monthly.*

CONTENTS

FOREWORD

Elisabeth Kubler-Ross, M. D.

YEARS HAVE PASSED since I have seen Maidanek, one of the many concentration camps in Europe. I grew up in Switzerland —an island of peace surrounded by the holocaust of World War II and the rumor, later the knowledge, that concentration camps did indeed exist! The day the war was over I set out on a long journey to do relief work throughout devastated Europe. The ruined cities, the hungry children, the lonely widows were only a part of the memory that I shall carry with me for the rest of my life.

It was Maidanek—with its gas chambers and by then empty barracks, the scribbles on the walls by children who died there, and the ever-present smell that refused to disappear — which ultimately led me to study death and dying. It was the train-loads of baby shoes, taken from the victims, the boxes of jewelry and women's hair that led to the ultimate questions: What is man? Where was God?

Ultimately, it is the knowledge of our own potential destruc-tiveness that forces us today to confront ourselves with the meaning of life and death. With the end of the war came hope — Israel was born — a promise of freedom and more hope, but this too was a dream: bombs decimated Hiroshima and Nagasaki, forests and fruitful lands were obliterated in Viet-nam, more young people died in Southeast Asia and the Middle East, children starved in Biafra and Bangladesh. And

1

we have finally reached the point where we have no choice but to re-evaluate our values and goals, lest we destroy ourselves and any possibility of a future for our children.

In the last decades, many books have been written on death and dying. Robert J. Lifton, probably the most outstanding scientist and writer on this topic, confronts us boldly with the consequences of our own destructiveness. Similarly, Joseph Rheingold, perhaps the only man ever to study the origin of our fear of death on an individual level, came to the conclusion that it is ultimately fear of our own destructiveness that plagues our every day of life.

I have always wondered why the Jews as a people have not written more on death and dying. Who, better than they, could contribute to our understanding of the need to face the reality of our own finiteness? It is Jewish people who have suffered more than any others over the centuries, who have been faced with more threats and attempts at their annihilation — not simply as individuals, but for them all as "Children of Israel."

Now it is with great pride and appreciation that I contribute in a small way to this book written by Jewish people, to join the many who have followed my own work and that of others to become allies and disciples in this humble attempt: To do something before it is too late.

Jewish Reflections on Death is a much-needed and appreciated contribution to our present discussion of life and death. Reading Rabbi Riemer's own essay, I could not help but wish that all people would observe a special day of awareness once a year, that all people would wear shrouds on that day — as Jews do on Yom Kippur — to remind ourselves that *today* counts, to make us aware that the deeds of today determine the degree of peace that we will find when we leave this life.

The articles in this collection speak with wisdom, compassion, and insight, and behind each of them stands a tradition so old, so rich in experience, and so humane as to be in itself a testament to the enduring value of its response to life as well as to death. Elie Wiesel's description of the death of his father is perhaps the most moving document of our times. It is complemented by Hans J. Morgenthau's essay on sacrificial death as an outgrowth of individual decision, in contrast to the slaughter of innocents — the millions of Jews in Buchenwald, Auschwitz, and Maidanek (to name only the most notorious examples), and the constant threat of nuclear destruction that shadows our modern times. Hayim Greenberg's "The Right to Kill" forces us again to face the dilemma of euthanasia, and I read with great relief that he does not join the ever-growing ranks of people who are ready to kill with the rationalization that this is an act of love.

Let us hope that this book assists many more people to become aware that "death then is not simply man's coming to an end. It is also a beginning" (Abraham J. Heschel). I hope, as much, that we have in some way begun to renew our respect for life, love, caring, and compassion, and thus that we will be able to end the era of mass murder and destructiveness before it is too late.

INTRODUCTION: MODERNITY AND THE JEWISH WAY OF DEATH

1

A DEAR FRIEND OF MINE observes the anniversary of his father's death each year on the seventh day of Passover. We sat together one year reminiscing about his father, and he recalled to me his memories of the last day of his father's life. His father was conscious until near the end, and so, knowing that it was a festival, he said his prayers including the Hallel, the psalms of thanksgiving and rejoicing. When he finished reciting the Hallel he felt weary and so he said the Vidui, the confessional. Soon afterward he died.

I was very moved by that recollection. To think that a man could bring his days to an end with the songs of the Hallel on his lips! What a fitting way to leave! I wonder which words of the Hallel spoke most directly to his heart on that last day of his life. Was it a phrase like:

> Grievous in the sight of the Lord
> Is the death of His faithful ones.

or was it perhaps a line like:

> What shall I give back to the Lord
> For all of His goodness to me?

5

Was it a phrase like:

> Answer me, O Lord, for I am Your servant,
> I am Your servant, the child of Your handmaid,
> Undo my chains

or was it perhaps the line:

> From the narrow place I cried out: "Lord!"
> He answered me with great enlargement.

We will never know, for we can no longer ask him. We can only speculate as to which of the words of the Hallel meant the most to my friend's father on the last day that he said them. But we can envy and be impressed with a man who was able to summarize his life at the end in ancient, hallowed words of thanksgiving and rejoicing. And we can envy and be impressed with the son who is fortunate enough to have these as his last memories of a parent.

2

It is highly unlikely that very many of us will ever be able to remember loved ones departing this life with such appropriate words as the words of the Hallel, or for that matter with any words at all. And this for two reasons. One is medical technology, the other is medical mythology.

Medical technology now makes it almost impossible for anyone to hear or to say any last words. The new drugs and sedatives kill the pain, but they also diminish the consciousness. They blur the mind and make communication very difficult. And the intensive-care units in which most people pass away now are not equipped for communication. Visitors can stay there only for a few minutes each hour, and while they do, they feel like intruders amid all the strange gadgets and complex machinery that are at work there. Most people perish in isolation now, unable to share a word or feel a comforting hand in theirs when the end comes.

Medical mythology plays its part in making death a lonely experience too. By medical mythology I mean the understandable squeamishness of doctors and nurses and attendants who share the same fears and phobias that all people have about death and who therefore tend to avoid it or deny it. For doctors who have been trained to fight to save and enhance life, each patient's death is a kind of defeat, and so it is understandable that they find it hard to accept. Doctors are faced with the unhappy choice of either becoming accustomed to death so that they can survive emotionally the strain of their work and thereby becoming callous, or else of letting themselves be torn apart by feelings of failure and grief and guilt with each patient whom they lose. And nurses understandably prefer to concentrate on those patients who are able to respond to and appreciate their ministerings and to avoid those patients who are soon about to die. And so a conspiracy of silence sets in around the terminally ill patient. No one wants to tell him what he has, no one wants to face his questions, no one wants to look into his eyes for fear of seeing one's own mortality reflected there. And so we avoid them, and they die alone.

These two images — of the man who died with the Hallel on his lips and of the man who died attached to tubes and wires — express the dilemma which is death in our time. The former came to his end while in relationship to those who had gone before him; their wisdom and their words were on his lips, and he left an image and a lesson and a model in his going for those who would come after him. The latter died alone, in sterile, antiseptic isolation.

3

Dr. Elisabeth Kubler-Ross, the woman whose work with terminally ill patients has probably done more than anyone else's to bring about a revolution in our understanding of their needs, says that when she first began her work she encountered enormous resistance from fellow members of the healing professions. She tells of how she would go looking from ward to ward in one large metropolitan hospital in search of terminally ill patients whom she could interview only to be told in every case that this ward did not have any such patients. It soon became clear to her that the doctors, the nurses, the chaplains, the hospital staff, and the relatives of the patients on these wards were all involved in an act of self-deception, and that they needed as much help in coping with their feelings and their fears as did the patients themselves. And so now she conducts seminars and study groups in the hospitals in which the seriously ill teach by telling what their innermost needs and concerns are. Rather than resisting, as their doctors said they would, she finds that most patients welcome the opportunity to be of help to others and the chance to share their insights. And doctors, nurses, chaplains, and hospital staff members listen and learn and try to work out their own feelings about death.

People have been dying ever since the beginning of time, and yet we know so very little about it. People have been dying ever since the world began, and yet each one of us clings to the illusion that death is something that happens to other people but not to us.

It is out of a desire to confront this reality and to learn from it that this book is undertaken. If Judaism is, as we so often claim, a religion that speaks to all of life, then surely it must speak to death as well, for death is an inexorable part of life. If Judaism is a tradition that possesses any insights and perspectives on this, then surely we wish to know what they are, for this is the place where we all stand in darkness and crave for light. If Judaism has wisdom and guidance to offer us here, then surely we wish to hear it, for we know that no one can claim to be wise about life whose wisdom does not include a relationship to death.

There seems to be a new openness to the question of death in our time, especially among young people. Harvard recently announced a seminar on death and arranged for it to meet in a room with twenty chairs. More than two hundred students showed up for the first session! The same kind of experience is being recorded on other campuses as well. A few years ago death was a great unmentionable, something that was covered over with euphemisms and disguised with all kinds of self-deceptions. It was treated in much the same way that sex was once treated by the Victorians, as something that we all knew existed but that was never to be talked about in public. Now there seems to be a different mood. Young people are more open, more willing to confront mortality, more able to understand that death is a dimension and a constant companion of life.

In the seminars and the study groups that are now taking place on campus, death is studied from many different points of view. There are courses on death in modern psychoanalysis, death in contemporary fiction and poetry, death in existentialism, death in the modern movie, and death in Christian thought. This book is an effort to add some Jewish points of view to the discussion, for surely a people that has lived as long and thought as hard as has the Jewish people must have some wisdom to contribute from out of its experience.

4

The Jewish way of death is different, just as the Jewish way of life is different. To capture it in a couple of phrases is impossible. Every summary is a distortion. But there are certain underlying principles that can be stated. Among them are these:

Judaism is realistic. It knows that death is part of each man's life, and it knows that self-deception does no good. So in the Bible the patriarchs face up to the fact of death with simple honesty. "Behold I am now about to go in the way of all the earth," says David to his son, and "Behold I am now about to die," says Joseph to his brothers. It is as simple, as painful, and as undeniable as that.

This realism about death and about the need to know it and prepare for it all the days of one's life is a motif that can be traced all the way through the tradition. So, for example, on the Day of Atonement the tradition bids a person don the kittel, the plain white linen garment that is at once both the symbol of freedom and status and also the shroud that he will wear at the end of his days. It is a humbling and a chastening thing to wear one's shroud once a year. It makes one realize that his days are numbered and that they are flying by. That man you mean to visit one of these days, that former friend you have been quarreling with, they too stand before the Lord this day wearing the kittel. The sight of them dressed this way is a vivid reminder that "one of these days" may be too late, and that if you have someone to love, someone to make up with, or someone to help, you had better do it now.

The Day of Atonement can be understood in part as a kind of annual encounter with or rehearsal for death. The person who on this day lets go of all his ordinary pleasures and possessions, who on this day touches no food or drink, who on this day blesses his children as if in farewell, and who on this day takes seriously the liturgy with all its stress on man's frailty, feels his mortality as on no other day.

A second example of realism is the section of prayers to be said when dying that is found in the classic prayer book. The prayer book that spoke to and regulated all the other moments of life had a section of prayers to be said at the last moments of life as well. The section was brief and simple, the words were plain and direct, but they contain a certain grace and wisdom and they are worth our study.

The first lines were honest and yet optimistic:

> I acknowledge before Thee, O Lord my God and God of my fathers, that my life and my death are in Thy hands. May it be Thy will to heal me. But if death is my lot, then I accept it from Thy hand with love.

Then came a simple confession of sin and a prayer expressing trust in God's goodness:

> May my death be an atonement for whatever sins and errors and wrongdoings I have committed before Thee. In Thy mercy grant me of the goodness that is waiting for the righteous, and bring me to eternal life.

> Father of the orphans, Protector of the widows, protect my loved ones with whom my soul is bound.

And it ended with these simple words of trust:

> Into Thy hands I return my spirit. Thou wilt redeem me, O ever faithful God.
> Hear O Israel, the Lord our God, the Lord is One.

It is unfortunate that this page has fallen out of our modern prayer books and that it is nowhere taught in the curricula of many of our religious schools. We cheat our children if we do not let them know of the existence of this part of their heritage. I simply cannot comprehend why we spend so many weeks and months teaching them how to become Bar or Bat Mitzvah and never spend an hour teaching them this page, as if they will never need to know it.

I suppose it is part of the general resistance of parents who fight to shield their children from contact with sorrow and from knowledge of death. We say that the world is bitter enough already without laying any additional burdens upon them before they need to have them. We tell ourselves: Let them confront death when they must, and not at a time when they are still so sensitive and so tender.

That would be tenable if we could arrange our lives so that everything happened at its appointed time. Unfortunately, fate is not such an obedient servant. Therefore we would be much wiser and much kinder to our children if we helped prepare them to face death before they need to know about it. This page of the prayer book is not morbid but realistic, and we have diminished the power of the prayer book considerably by deleting it from our modern editions.

Another precious Jewish practice that has unfortunately been nearly lost in modern times is the writing of an ethical will. People today use lawyers and banks and trust experts to make sure that their financial affairs will be in order after they are gone. Our ancestors had less property to be concerned about but they were concerned that their values continue. And so they wrote ethical wills to leave behind for their children, wills in which they tried to summarize the faith they had lived by and the goals they wanted their children to cherish. Some of these wills from Talmudic and medieval times have been collected by Israel Abrahams and published in a beautiful bilingual edition by the Jewish Publication Society. One modern example of an ethical will is the last word of this book. It was written by a man to his children at a time when he was well and put aside until the time when they would need to read it. It remains now as a beautiful statement for them, and for us who are permitted to share it with them, of what this man stood for and believed in.

Perhaps more of us ought to do what this man did and set down in words an ethical will so our children may have a document that will tell them who we were and what we stood for, what we tried to impart to them, and what we hoped and prayed and wanted for them and from them after we are gone. One does not need to be an elegant stylist or a profound philosopher to write such a will. "Words that come from the heart enter the heart," as the Talmud says, and sincerity more than makes up for lack of writing skill. An ethical will is a good thing to leave behind.

There are many more facets to the Jewish way of dying. There is the halakhah, that great and complex and immensely detailed system of law that gives form and order and structure to our grief and keeps it from becoming wild or shapeless or uncontrolled. There is the community, which shares in the joys and sorrows of every individual Jew and makes of the rites of passage in his life events in the history of the whole Jewish people from Abraham to the end of time. The community reaches out to the Jew in his time of grief and lets him know that he is not alone and not abandoned. His first food is prepared for him by others, for otherwise he might not remember to eat, and to eat means to go on living. The synagogue moves to his home and the services are held there during the seven days of mourning so that he feels himself a part of the community at the time of his greatest isolation. And for the year that follows he does not pray in private but in the company of the minyan, as a member of the "fraternity of mourners" who come together twice each day. In an age such as ours when constant mobility has weakened the sense of neighborhood, and family ties are so attenuated, and anonymity is so great, the sense of community that the Jewish mourning laws provide may be one of their greatest blessings.

Community, as Jews understand it, is not only horizontal but vertical as well. The biblical phrase for dying is "to be gathered to one's people" or "to be gathered to his fathers." One becomes a part of history when he dies. And one of the meanings of the Kaddish is that one becomes an ancestor, and one is linked and bound up with those who come afterward.

There is realism, there is halakhah, there is community, and there is God. God is the partner and the source of life and also of death. It is God who makes of death a homecoming and a return. God is the mystery from whom we come and to whom we go. He is the mystery that towers above all our questions about death and who towers above all our answers about death. As Abraham J. Heschel wrote: "Eternity is the memory of God. Creative insights grow a lifetime to last a moment, and yet they last forever. For to last means to commune with God, 'to cleave to Him.' Within eternity every moment can become a contemporary of God. Eternity is not perpetual future but perpetual presence."

Realism, halakhah, community, God — these are some of the facets of the Jewish way of death as it has come down to us through the centuries. Each of these has been shaken and almost shattered by the impact of modernity. It is our desire in this book to determine how much of this tradition still remains valid despite modernity, and how much remains even more valid because of the special conditions that constitute modernity.

5

The essays in this book are all modern Jewish reflections on death. What makes them Jewish is that they are all by people who have come out of the Jewish tradition, who have been shaped at least in part by it, and who strive to understand and transmit it. What makes them modern is that they are all by people who wrestle with that tradition all the days of their lives in the light of the moods and the mentality of our time.

Modernity means many different things to these writers, but for all of them it is a challenge. For Emanuel Feldman modernity means knowing the findings and the methods of anthropology and sociology and having to see the tradition in that perspective. For Elie Wiesel modernity means Auschwitz, with all that that word implies. It means confronting a broken universe, one in which both simple faith and simple atheism are now impossible. It means striving to pick up the pieces after the catastrophe and trying to restore some meaning and order and continuity once again after the break. For Abraham Kaplan and Daniel Jeremy Silver modernity means the new achievements of medical science and technology, which raise unprecedented questions that require new answers. No one before our time had to rule on such questions as transplants or the precise definition of death or whether tubes and machines and heroic efforts are really preserving life or only preserving the process of dying. But medical technology has made these questions real, and so they must be answered. For Hans J. Morgenthau modernity means the Bomb, which for the first time in human history brings the survival of the planet itself into question. For Morris Adler modernity means an increasingly atomized society in which men live in apartment houses or on suburban estates and never get to know each other, and feel the need for some sense of community. For Hayim Greenberg modernity means the challenge of a materialistic world view in which the achievement of pleasure and the avoidance of pain have become the measures of life. And for Joseph B. Soloveitchik, a man for whom the law has transcendent meaning and eternal validity, modernity means an age in which the sense of law has been lost and has been replaced by custom, opinion, whim, and fad.

Each of the authors in this collection stands between two worlds. They are all, in greater or lesser degree, products of the Jewish tradition and students of its meaning. But they are also in every single case citizens of the modern world with all its blessings and all its problems. They have been shaped, each of them, by modernity as well as by tradition. In these essays they seek to reconcile the two. They do two things in every essay. They confront the tradition critically from the perspective of our time, and they confront our time, its values and its premises, from the perspective of the tradition.

No one is an expert on death and no one should pretend to be. This is something that each of us must learn and experience by and for himself. But we can strengthen and enlighten each other. We can learn from the wisdom and experience of each other and from the wisdom and experience of those who have gone before us. It is to this sharing and this strengthening and this search that this book is dedicated.

J. R.

PRELUDE

Before Modernity

As a prelude to to the study of what death means in modern Jewish thought and experience, we present first two selections concerning death and mourning from premodern Jewish literature, one from the halakhah, and one from the haggadah.

Halakhah and haggadah are the two great subdivisions of Jewish religious writing. They are usually translated as "law" and as "legend." Halakhah is the effort to give form to all of life; haggadah is the effort to convey the spirit within the form.

As an example of halakhah we have chosen some excerpts from the sections on death and mourning in the Shulhan Aruk. As an example of haggadah we have chosen some excerpts from a Hasidic text called *Histalkut Hanefesh.*

The Shulhan Aruk was compiled by Rabbi Joseph Karo of Safed in the sixteenth century. The glosses that accompany almost every paragraph in it are the work of Rabbi Moses Isserles of Kracow. It was Isserles who gave Karo's work status and authority by adding to its summation of the Sephardic traditions those of the Ashkenazic community. The sections of mourning in the Shulhan Aruk are actually much longer and much more technical than this brief sampling can indicate. Each paragraph included here has subdivisions, glosses, fine points, and commentaries in the original that we have had to screen out because of their technical nature. And the Shulhan Aruk itself must be understood, not as the final arbiter, but as one stage in the continuing exposition of the law and the study of its application to new situations which goes on in the responsa literature and the commentaries of every generation up to and including our own.

15

For the halakhah there is no such thing as the ordinary, or the secular, or the trivial. Ethics, values, and principles are never allowed to be left as generalities; they must be crystallized into norms. Always the debate is phrased, not in the abstract, but in terms of "What should we do?" and in terms of the most minute details.

Haggadah is an entirely different kind of writing and thinking. Not bound to the mundane, it can soar toward the sky. While halakhah deals with those things that can be measured, defined, and expressed literally, haggadah introduces us to a realm that lies beyond the range of expression.

For the example of haggadah we have chosen a document from Hasidic literature. Hasidism was the last great spiritual movement of the Jewish Middle Ages. It arose as the Jewish people stood on the threshold of modernity. It derived its power not only from its profound ideas but from the sense of community that it developed among its adherents and from the intense, loving relationship between the leaders and their disciples which characterized it. For Hasidim their leaders were not only teachers but models. They felt that there was wisdom to be learned not only from their words but also from observing the way they lived, and even from the way they died. They sensed that the way in which a man meets death is the product of the way in which he has lived life. If we have lived a life of futility and pointlessness, then we are bound to meet our end with anger and resentment. If we have lived our lives in faith, then we can meet our end in trust. If we have lived our lives in devotion and service, then we are able to meet our end with gratitude and a sense of completion. To record the last moments of their masters was for the Hasidim a sacred task. It meant more than just to record these last few moments. It meant to capture a whole lifetime in a symbol, a whole spirit in a word, a whole philosophy in a gesture, and then to become the witness and the teller of that tale and the transmitter of that insight to those who would come after. One such collection by Hasidim of the way their teachers died is *Histalkut Hanefesh*, edited by Benjamin Mintz in 1930, from which these excerpts have been translated.

1

FROM THE SHULHAN ARUK

Translated by Chaim N. Denburg

(From Chapter 335: When to visit the sick, which sick persons should be visited, and how to pray for the sick.)

1. It is a religious duty to visit the sick. Relatives and close friends should enter at once, others after three days. If the illness is serious, both groups can visit him at once.

2. Even a distinguished person should visit a humble one. The more one visits the more praiseworthy it is, provided only that the visits do not become a burden to the patient.

Gloss: Some say that an enemy may not visit a sick person. However, this does not seem plausible to me. But he should not visit a sick person whom he hates lest the patient think that he is rejoicing at his misfortune and become depressed.

3. One who visits the sick should not sit upon a bed or upon a chair or upon a stool but should sit in front of the patient, for the Divine Presence rests above a sick person.

Gloss: This applies only if the patient lies upon the ground, but if the patient lies upon a bed then it is permissible for the visitor to sit upon a chair or a stool. And this is our custom.

4. One should not visit the sick during the first three hours of the day, for every patient's illness is alleviated in the morning, and consequently he will not trouble himself to pray for him; and not during the last three hours of the day, for then his illness grows worse and one will give up hope to pray for him.

Gloss: One who visited a sick person and did not pray for him has not fulfilled his religious duty.

5. When one prays for him, if in his presence, one may pray in any language; if not in his presence, one should pray in Hebrew.

6. When praying for a sick person one should combine him with all the others who are ill by saying: "May the Omnipresent have mercy upon you together with all the rest of the sick in Israel." On the Sabbath one should say: "This is the Sabbath when one must not cry and yet may recovery come soon."

7. The sick person should be advised to look over his affairs and to see if he has any debts or credits outstanding. He should be reassured that this is only a precaution and that it does not mean that he is about to die.

8. One should not visit those who are suffering from those diseases where a visit will cause the patient embarrassment or discomfort. If a person is so ill that conversation is a strain to him, he should not be visited, but instead one should stand in the antechamber and inquire about him, and offer whatever household or nursing help he may need, and sympathize with him, and pray for him.

(From Chapter 338: The sick person's confessional.)

1. When death draws near he is advised to confess. And we reassure him: "Many have confessed and then not died just as many have not confessed and died." If he is unable to confess aloud let him confess in his heart. If he does not know what to say we instruct him to say: "May my death be an expiation for all my sins." This is not done in the presence of women and children lest they cry and break his heart.

2. The order of the confessional for a terminally ill person is set.*

Gloss: But if he wishes he has the right to say more, even as much as the long confessional of the Day of Atonement.

(From Chapter 339: Laws concerning one who is dying.)

1. One who is dying is considered a living being in all respects. We may not tie up his jaws, nor remove the pillow from under him, nor place him on sand, nor summon the town on

*For the text of the confessional see the Introduction, page 10.

his behalf, nor close his eyes before his soul departs. And whoever closes his eyes before death, is regarded as a murderer.
One may not rend garments nor make a lamentation for him
nor bring a coffin into the house for him before he dies.

Gloss: Some say that we may not dig a grave for him before
he dies even though this is not done in his presence and he
would not be aware of it. It is likewise forbidden to hasten the
death of a dying man — e.g., if one has been moribund for a
long time and continues to linger on, we may not remove the
pillow or the mattress from under him or do anything overt to
hasten his death. However, if there is anything external that
prevents his release from his death pangs, such as a clattering
noise near the patient's house, or if there is salt on his tongue,
and these hinder the departure of the soul, it is permitted to
remove them, for this is no direct act but only the removal of a
hindrance.

4. When a person is about to die one should not leave him
so that he does not depart this life alone.

Gloss: It is a *mitzvah* to stand by a person during the departure of his soul.

(From Chapter 340: The laws of cutting *keriah.)*

1. Whoever has suffered a bereavement for which he is required to observe the mourning rites must cut his garments.
One must do so standing, and if he did so while sitting he has
not fulfilled his duty.

2. The region for rending is all along the neck of the garment in the forepart. If he rent in the back part or in the lower
part of the garment or on the side, he has not discharged his
duty.

3. The extent of rending is a handbreadth. If he rent his
garment upon suffering a bereavement and then extended the
rent on sustaining another bereavement, if the second bereavement is after the seven days of mourning, then the additional tear may be as small as he wishes.

(From Chapter 343: The duty of attending the dead to the
grave.)

1. So long as there is a dead person in town awaiting burial
all the townspeople are forbidden to engage in work. And
whoever sees a corpse and does not attend to its needs is sub-

ject to being placed under a ban. However, if there are associations in town, each one of which attends to the burial needs of the dead on its particular day, then it is permissible for the others who are not required to attend to the burial needs to engage in work on the day which is not appointed for it.

(From Chapter 345: The law regarding one who commits suicide.)

1. One who commits suicide willfully is not attended to at all. One does not mourn for him, no lamentation is made for him, nor does one rend garments for him. But one does stand in the line to give comfort to the mourners for him and one does recite for him the mourner's blessing. Whatever is done for the sake of the mourners we do, whatever is done for the sake of the dead we do not do.

2. Who is considered a suicide? For example, if one announced that he is going to go up to the rooftop and jump and they saw him go up at once in anger or distress and fall from there, such a person is considered a deliberate suicide. But if he is found strangled or pierced with a sword, he is presumed to be like all other dead and we attend to him and withhold nothing from him.

3. A child who commits suicide deliberately is considered as if he had done it unintentionally. And likewise, one who was under pressure, as King Saul was, we consider it unintentional, and we hold back nothing from him.

(From Chapter 349: Whoever throws recklessly many garments upon the dead commits the sin of "Do not waste." From Chapter 352: Laws concerning the garments in which the dead are buried.)

1. The corpse is not buried in expensive shrouds even if he be the Prince of Israel.

2. The accepted custom is to bury the dead in white garments.

3. A man should not wrap or tie burial garments around a woman.

4. One closes the eyes of the dead, and if his mouth opens, one ties up the jaws and stops off the organs of the extremities.

Gloss: And one washes him thoroughly all over so that he be clean of all impurity.

(From Chapter 360: In case of a conflict between the religious duty of escorting a corpse and the religious duty of honoring a bride.)

1. If a funeral procession and a bridal procession meet each other on the way, the funeral procession should make way for the bridal procession. Likewise, if there are not enough people in the city to attend both, they bring the bride under the canopy first and then they bury the dead. But after the wedding ceremony, if a man has the duty to comfort the mourner and to gladden the bride and groom, comforting the mourner comes first. Similarly, the mourner's meal takes precedence over the wedding feast. When does this rule apply? When he has the means to fulfill both obligations; but if he does not possess the means to fulfill both, then the wedding feast comes first.

In the case of a corpse and a circumcision, circumcision comes first. If, however, he is a corpse that has no attendants at all, then he has priority over all else.

(From Chapter 376: On how to behave at the house of mourning.)

1. The comforters should not speak until the mourner initiates the conversation. When the mourner nods his head, indicating that he dismisses the comforters, they should not remain with him any longer.

Gloss: A mourner is not required to rise in honor of any distinguished visitor even if it be the leader of all Israel.

(From Chapter 378: The laws of the mourner's meal.)

1. A mourner is forbidden to eat of his own food at the first meal upon return from the burial. Some explain that this is because sometimes the mourner refuses to eat and prefers death; the meal provided by the neighbors is thus an act of assisting the bereaved toward reaccepting life.

10. A great number of people should not assemble to eat with the mourner, for this would necessitate that they overflow into two groups.

(From Chapter 380. Things forbidden to the mourner.)

1. The following are the things forbidden to the mourner: He is forbidden to engage in work, to bathe, to anoint himself, to put on shoes, to have marital intercourse, to read the Pen-

tateuch, to greet one, to wash his garments during the first seven days of mourning and to cut his hair, to rejoice, and to resew a rent during the whole of the thirty days of mourning.

2. To what extent is a mourner forbidden to engage in work? During the first three days he is forbidden to engage in work even if he is a poor man who is supported from charity. Thereafter, if he is a poor man and has nothing to eat, he may work in the privacy of his house. But the Sages say: May poverty come upon his community who by not providing his maintenance at such a time were the cause of his needing to engage in work.

6. A woman should not paint her eyelids nor rouge her face during the days of her mourning. A married woman is forbidden to do this only during the seven days, but after this she is permitted everything so that she will not become repulsive in the sight of her husband. A bride whose mourning befell within the thirty days subsequent to her marriage is permitted to adorn herself even within the first seven days. A girl who has reached adolescence whom mourning befalls is permitted to paint her eyelids and apply rouge to her face but does not bathe her entire body in warm water. A girl who has not reached adolescence and who becomes a mourner is forbidden even painting of the eyelids and applying rouge to her face.

(From Chapter 382: The prohibition concerning shoes.)

1. A mourner is forbidden to put on shoes only if they are made of leather, but a pair of shoes made of cloth, reeds, hair, or wood is permitted. However, if it was made of wood and covered over with leather, it is forbidden.

2. A woman after confinement, or a pregnant woman, or one who is ill, or one who has a wound on her foot, is permitted to wear leather shoes because the cold may be harmful to her.

(From Chapter 384: On the study of Torah.)

1. A mourner during the seven days is forbidden to study the Pentateuch, Prophets, or Hagiographa, or Mishnah, Gemara, halakhah, or haggadah. If, however, the community has need of him, he is permitted.

4. A mourner is permitted to read Job, Lamentations, the sad parts of Jeremiah, or the Laws of Mourning.

(From Chapter 394: On grieving excessively.)

1. One should not grieve too much for the dead, and whoever grieves excessively is really grieving for someone else. The Torah has set limits for every stage of grief, and we may not add to them: three for weeping, seven for lamenting, and thirty for abstaining from laundered garments and from cutting the hair — and no more.

6. Whoever does not mourn as the law has prescribed is considered callous. Instead, when a loss occurs, a person should tremble and fear and examine his deeds, and above all he should repent and return and change his ways.

2

THE DEATHS OF THE HASIDIC MASTERS (From the *Histalkut Hanefesh*)

Translated by Samuel H. Dresner

WHEN THE HOUR ARRIVED for Rabbi Simhah Bunam of Psyshcha to depart from the world, his wife stood by his bedside and wept bitterly. He said to her, "Be silent — why do you cry? My whole life was only that I might learn how to die." He died on the twelfth day of Elul, 1827.

Before the death of Rabbi Abraham Joshua Heschel of Apt, he moaned bitterly over the exile of his people and over the fact that the Messiah tarried in coming. Finally he cried out, "The Rabbi of Berditchev said before he died that when he arrived up there he would not rest nor be silent, nor would he allow any of the holy ones to rest or be silent until the Messiah would come. But when he came there, the beauties and wonders of heaven overwhelmed him, so that he forgot about this. But I" — concluded the Rabbi of Apt — "I shall not forget."

Afterward he said: "Master of the world, I know that I am not worthy to be allowed to enter heaven with the other righteous men. Perhaps you will permit me to enter Gehenna with the wicked. But you, O Master of the World, you know how much I hate those who transgress your will. You know I cannot bear to be with them. How should I then make my dwelling among them? Therefore, I beg of you that you remove all the wicked of Israel from Gehenna in order that you might be able to bring me there." He died on the fifth of Nissan, 1825.

Rabbi Sussya of Plozk raised his head at midnight and said, "At midnight I rise to praise Thee," and with these words his soul departed from him. He died in the year 1840.

Rabbi Mayer, the son of Eliezer of Dzikov, died while he was sitting on his chair with his pipe in his mouth. He said, "The soul is Thine and the body is Thy work. Have mercy upon Thy craft." And when he had finished these words, his pure soul departed. He died on the eighth day of Tammuz, 1876.

It is told that Rabbi Abi of Olinov was among the greatest admirers of Rabbi Naphtali of Ropshitz. He died on Simchat Torah in Olinov. At that time, the Hasidim in Ropshitz were dancing in their fashion before the window of their Rabbi. Rabbi Naphtali stood by the window and watched. Suddenly he raised his hand as a sign that they should stop. And he stood as if in confusion for some time. Afterward he roused himself and said, "If they go out to war and one of the captains falls, should the soldiers flee? No. The battle must go on. Rejoice and dance." Then he gave a sign that they should begin to dance. Afterward it was made known that this was the precise moment when Rabbi Abi had died.

In the year 1831 a terrible plague raged in the world, and many letters were sent to Rabbi Zvi Hirsch of Ziditchov, from many distant places, saying: "O Rabbi, save us." One day when many of these letters were handed to him, and he was robed in his tallit, while he stood in his house of study, he grieved greatly, put his hand upon the *mezzuzah,* and said, "Behold, I shall be a *kapparah* [atonement] for all Israel." On the next Sabbath, when he put on his tallit, he saw that one fringe was torn and said, "It needs to be renewed." On the next Sabbath, his wife died. Then he himself fell ill and was no longer able to rise from his bed. On the tenth of Tammuz, a serious illness seized him. He asked his son-in-law if it was permissible for a man to look for a virtue within himself. His son-in-law said that, according to the Torah, it was permissible. He said, "I have served through the length of my days and I have only found one virtue among them: that I married off forty orphans. Each time I married off one of my own children, grandchildren, nieces, or nephews, I married off an orphan girl and provided her with a dowry and food at my own table."

At the hour of the death of the Ari, all of his students gathered around him with the exception of Rabbi Hayim Vital. Rabbi Isaac Hacohen [the priest] cried out, "Is this to be our hope, for all of us have waited to see great goodness and Torah and wisdom in the world while you yet live?" The Ari answered, "If I had found even one true zaddik among you, I would not depart." Afterward he inquired, "Where is Rabbi Hayim Vital?" And he seemed troubled. It was evident from the manner of his words that he wanted to hand over some secret to him. Later on, they inquired of him, "What shall we do from this time forth?" The Ari said, "You shall say to the disciples, in my name, that from this time forth they should not study Cabbala at all, for they have not understood it properly, and they might come, God forbid, to doubt and even to the destruction of their souls. Only Rabbi Hayim Vital may study it, in secret." The disciples asked, "Is there then no hope for us?" "If you merit it," he replied, "I myself shall come and teach you." Rabbi Isaac Hacohen asked, "How shall our Rabbi come to teach us after he has departed from the world?" He said, "It is not for you to delve into secret things, how I shall come — whether by night or by day, or in a vision. And now rise up quickly and leave this house for you are a priest [and forbidden to be in the same room with a dead man]; the time has come and I cannot speak more about this matter."

Rabbi Isaac rose to take leave at once, but before he had gone out of the door, the Ari opened his mouth and his soul departed with a kiss. He died on the fifth of Ab, 1605.

When the Baal Shem Tov fell ill shortly before his death, he would not take to bed. His body grew weak, his voice faint, and he would sit alone in his room meditating. On the eve of Shabuot, the last evening of his life, his intimates were gathered around him and he preached to them about the giving of the Torah. In the morning he requested that all of them gather together in his room and he taught them how they should care for his body after death. Afterward he asked for a Siddur [prayer book] and said, "I wish to commune yet a while with *Hashem Yitbarakh* [the Name, may He be blessed]."

Afterward they heard him talking to someone and they inquired with whom he was speaking. He replied, "Do you not see the Angel of Death? He always flees from me, but now he has been given permission to come and flaps his wings and is full of joy." Afterward all the men of the city gathered together to greet him on the holiday and he spoke words of Torah to them. Afterward he said, "Until now I have treated you with *hesed* [loving kindness]. Now you must treat me with *hesed*." [The burial is considered the truest act of *hesed*, because there is no repayment.] He gave them a sign that at his death the two clocks in the house would stop.

While he was washing his hands, the large clock stopped and some of the men immediately stood in front of it so that the others should not see it. He said to them, "I am not worried about myself, for I know clearly that I shall go from this door and immediately I shall enter another door." He sat down on his bed and told them to stand around him. He spoke words of Torah and ordered them to recite the verse — "And let Thy graciousness, O Lord our God, be upon us; establish Thou also the work of our hands for us; Yea the work of our hands establish Thou it." He lay down and sat up many times and prayed with great *kavvanah* and devotion, until the syllables of his words could no longer be distinguished. He told them to cover him with blankets and began to shake and tremble as he used to do when he prayed the Silent Prayer. Then little by little he grew quiet. At that moment they saw that the small clock too had stopped. They waited and saw that he had died. He died on Shabuot, 1760.

Before the great Maggid, Rabbi Dov Ber of Mezritch, departed from the world, there stood before him his son Rabbi Abraham, "the Angel," Rabbi Judah Leib, the priest, and Rabbi Shneer Zalman, the Rabbi from Ladi. He said to them, "My children, hold fast to one another in unity, for by this you will overcome everything. Go forward and not backward. Afterward the zaddik, Rabbi Zussya of Hanipol, entered, and he intimated to him with a gesture of his finger that he come close. He took his right hand and said to him, "You, Zussya, were mine in this world and there, too, you shall be close to me." Later on he inquired whether Rabbi Mendel of Vitebsk was there and groaned when he learned that he was not. He asked whether Rabbi Leib Cohen was there. When he saw him he said to him, "You, too, shall be with me." Later he uttered these words, "Zalman, Zalman, you alone shall remain, but I shall take you out of your suffering and cause you to rejoice in the end." Then he said, "Abraham, you shall live. Only you shall be silent and conduct yourself as you have until now and serve Zalman — and it shall be good for you. The main thing is that you should not mortify yourself, for if you take from the strength of your body, you take also from the strength of your soul."

Then he said goodnight and he slept away. May his merit guard us all. He died on the nineteenth day of Kislev, 1774.

Rabbi Yehiel Michal of Zlotshov had already withdrawn completely from this world two years before his death, and it was necessary to watch over him carefully so that his soul should not depart from his body because of his great zeal in cleaving to the Creator. It was his habit to walk up and down in his room until his face would shine like a torch of flame. Especially then you had to watch him very carefully. It was his habit to eat the three meals alone with one of his sons in his room and afterward to walk to the House of Study to teach Torah and sing and pray to God. On the fatal day when he was taken from us, no one was with him in his room. He ran up and down, crying out, "In this manner Moses died — in this manner Moses died." His daughter heard him and brought her brother Rabbi Isaac. He hastened to the room, grasped him and shook him in order to bring him out of his ecstasy, but alas, it was too late. He fell upon his shoulder, recited Shema Yisrael, and with the word *Ehad*, ["one"] his soul departed. He died on the third of Nissan, 1786.

When the hour came for Rabbi Elimelekh to depart from the world, he placed his hands upon the foreheads of his four disciples and gave them each a portion of his soul. To the Seer of Lublin, he gave the light of his eyes. To the Maggid of Koshnitz, he gave his heart. To Rabbi Mendel of Prustik, he gave his mind. To the Rabbi of Apt, he gave the power of his tongue. He died on the twenty-first of Adar, 1786.

Many months before the death of Rabbi Nachman of Bratzlav — who already had achieved a rung so lofty that it seemed impossible to ascend higher while clothed with flesh — he said that he yearned to be free of his body. It was impossible for him to remain upon one rung for any length of time, for all of his days he had never stood still upon one rung even when he ascended to the highest point. He constantly yearned to go higher and higher. And so it was that a long time before he died he began to seek out a place of burial for himself, since for reasons he would not reveal, he did not wish to be buried in Bratzlav. At last he chose the city of Oman (where the Baal Shem, his grandfather, was born). He said that many deliverances could be brought about there and that there were many mysteries there which he could reveal to no one. When he settled in Oman, he had already grown very weak. On the Sabbath following Tishah-b'Ab, many Hasidim came to him and before they washed their hands for the meal, he said, "Why have you all come here? I do not know you at all, for I have now become a simple man."

On the last night of his life, he spoke again about the soul. He commanded his disciples that immediately after he had died, while he yet lay upon the earth, they should take all of his writings that were in his desk and burn them. He insisted that they carry out his command. They stood about in confusion and despair and whispered among themselves while he was already preparing himself to depart. Then he said to them, "Perhaps you are speaking about your own concerns. But why do you worry that I depart from you? If these souls who know me not at all, look to me for deliverance, how much the more so need you not fear." In the morning he gathered his tallit around him, prayed, took the ethrog and lulav, completed saying the Hallel in a strong voice, and used the siddur of the Ari, which rested upon his knees. Then he ordered them to dress

him and wash him. And he took some wax and rubbed it between his fingers and meditated great thoughts, as was the custom of the great men; when they would meditate about something they would turn over in their fingers some wax. Thus at
the last hour his mind was occupied with matters deep and
most wonderful.

And when they saw that it was close to the end, they began
to recite the verses which are said at the time of the death of
the righteous. When it appeared that he had died, they began
to cry out, "Our Rabbi — our Rabbi — with whom have you left
us?" At that moment he stirred, raised his head and his wonderful face as if to say, "I am not leaving you." Then he ex-
pired and was gathered to his people in holiness and in purity.
He died on the eighteenth day of Tishri, 1810.

Rabbi Aaron of Shtrashala, who took the place of Rabbi
Shneer Zalman, died on the evening of Shemini Atseret. On
Hoshana Rabba he prayed in his customary way, dancing happily during the hour of prayer, for then he was still healthy.
When he completed his worship at 4:00 in the afternoon, his
lulav was completely shattered. That evening he went to the
hakkafot. After the *hakkafot,* he lay down upon his bed and began
to expound on the verse, "On the eighth day He sent away the
people." And in the middle of the exposition, he said to Rabbi
Abraham that he should complete the sermon and he handed
over his soul in purity.

He died on the twenty-fifth of Tishri, 1833.

PART ONE

Two Modern Dilemmas and Two Responses

THE PREMODERN WORLD knew a full measure of complexity and tragedy. And yet it was characterized by a certain spiritual integrity that contrasts sharply with the modern temper. There were forms, clearly defined and generally accepted forms, with which to celebrate life and with which to commemorate death. And there was a faith, a many-sided and profound faith, that made life meaningful and death acceptable. In time of loss one knew what to do and one knew for whose sake.

Modernity has come at this tradition with a whole series of cruel and painful questions. Both the forms and the faith have become problematic. A whole series of new, unprecedented hammer blows have come down one after the other against the classic edifice of form and faith. Two of these challenges we identify with the symbolic names of Auschwitz and Hiroshima.

Auschwitz is a single term with which we symbolize a host of challenges to form and to faith that were involved in the Holocaust. Simple faith and simple atheism both went up in smoke there. Easy belief in God and easy belief in man were both dealt a grievous blow by what happened there. And so, as Elie Wiesel demonstrates here, we must wrestle with the question of what to do with the old forms now and of what to do with the old faith. Are the old rituals antedated, are they too naive, too innocent, too simple to still have any meaning after the Holocaust? Are there any new forms that the mind of man can fathom that will mean more? Are all words now too stained, and is even silence insufficient? Does what happened there represent such a break with all the past that continuing the old forms now seems mechanical? Or is this perhaps the only way in which to overcome the chasm and to respond to the horror? Auschwitz was the most systematic effort at dehumanization and degradation ever made. A whole technology was devised to make people feel that they were subhuman. Is the continuing of the old forms a way of resisting that dehumanization and of affirming man's roots and his rights and his personhood? Or is there perhaps no way to grieve, no way to mourn, no form that still speaks, after Auschwitz?

Hiroshima is another cluster word for a modern dilemma of immense proportion. Secular man had prided himself on having replaced the vision of salvation in some afterlife with a vision of salvation here on earth. It was by helping to make a better world for his heirs to enjoy that man was going to find his fulfillment and his immortality. But now, if the existence of the earth itself is problematic, if the implications of the Bomb and of the unsteady balance of the ecosphere fully penetrate our consciousness, if the planet itself is mortal, then what happens to man's immortality? What happens to such hallowed concepts as fame, honor, and memory if there will be no one left to honor and no one left to remember? What happens to our sense of self and to the worthwhileness of work and of life if the survival of the planet itself, within which these concepts have been located, becomes questionable? These are the issues that Hans J. Morgenthau confronts with so much anguish and so much honesty in his essay.

Deborah Lipstadt's essay can be understood in a certain sense as a response to Elie Wiesel's. The death of Elie Wiesel's father occurred in such a dark and dreadful place that it made any and all forms of observance seem gross, any and all ways of commemoration seem grotesque. Forms seemed an intrusion and an impertinence in the place of so much chaos. But the death of Deborah Lipstadt's father occurred in the midst of forms. It was the forms that gave order and structure and dignity to his going, as they had to his living, and it was the forms that gave guidance and strength to those whom he left behind. It was precisely the forms in all their abundance and all their wisdom that elevated him from being an individual and made him a link in the chain of the generations. It was the forms that defined him and gave him roots, and it was the forms that led his children through their grief and back into life. If Elie Wiesel's essay is a lament for the collapse of forms, Deborah Lipstadt's essay is a celebration of the saving power of forms.

Abraham J. Heschel's essay can be read in a certain sense as a response to the questions of Hans J. Morgenthau. No essay on death is ever academic. No matter how abstract or theoretical it may sound, no matter how impersonal and objective it may seem, and no matter how young and how healthy its author may feel himself to be, it is always written with an awareness that "we will someday be they." This essay is no exception. It was written by Abraham J. Heschel in the shadow of his first heart attack, and so it is no armchair theorizing but a personal confrontation.

What Hans J. Morgenthau is saying is that man's worth is thrown into question if the world on which his worth depends is finite. What Abraham J. Heschel is saying in his essay is that man is related, not only to the world, but also to "He who was before there was a world." "Man is man not only because of what he has in common with the earth but because of what he has in common with God. The Greek thinkers sought to understand man as a part of the universe; the Prophets sought to understand man as a partner of God."

Hans J. Morgenthau's essay is an exercise in realism, an unflinching confrontation with the grimmest possibility. Abraham J. Heschel's essay is an effort at vision. It is an attempt to see not only death but also life as a profound mystery. It is a warning against the kind of pedestrian existence that is a kind of death in life, and it is a plea for the kind of spirit that makes even of death a certain level of life. Morgenthau's essay is a modern apocalyptic, Heschel's a modern psalm of celebration. One plumbs the full horror of death; the other suggests its grandeur.

3

THE DEATH OF MY FATHER

By Elie Wiesel

THE ANNIVERSARY OF THE DEATH of a certain Shlomo ben Nissel falls on the eighteenth day of the month of Shebat. He was my father, the day is tomorrow; and this year, as every year since the event, I do not know how to link myself to it.

Yet, in the Shulhan Aruk, the great book of precepts by Rabbi Joseph Karo, the astonishing visionary-lawmaker of the sixteenth century, precise, rigorous rules on the subject do exist. I could and should simply conform to them. Obey tradition. Follow in the footsteps. Do what everyone does on such a day: Go to the synagogue three times, officiate at the service, study a chapter of Mishnah, say the orphan's Kaddish, and in the presence of the living community of Israel, proclaim the holiness of God as well as his greatness. For his ways are tortuous but just, his grace heavy to bear but indispensable, here on earth and beyond, today and forever. May his will be done. Amen.

This is undoubtedly what I would do had my father died of old age, of sickness, or even of despair. But such is not the case. His death did not even belong to him. I do not know to what cause to attribute it, in what book to inscribe it. No link between it and the life he had led. His death, lost among all the rest, had nothing to do with the person he had been. It could just as easily have brushed him in passing and spared him. It took him inadvertently, absentmindedly. By mistake. Without knowing that it was he; he was robbed of his death.

Stretched out on a plank of wood amid a multitude of blood-covered corpses, fear frozen in his eyes, a mask of suffering on the bearded, stricken mask that was his face, my father gave back his soul at Buchenwald. A soul useless in that place, and one he seemed to want to give back. But he gave it up, not to the God of his fathers, but rather to the impostor, cruel and insatiable, to the enemy God. They had killed his God, they had exchanged him for another. How, then, could I enter the sanctuary of the synagogue tomorrow and lose myself in the sacred repetition of the ritual without lying to myself, without lying to him? How could I act or think like everyone else, pretend that the death of my father holds a meaning calling for grief or indignation?

Perhaps, after all, I should go to the synagogue to praise the God of dead children, if only to provoke him by my own submission.

Tomorrow is the anniversary of the death of my father, and I am seeking a new law that prescribes for me what vows to make and no longer to make, what words to say and no longer to say.

In truth, I would know what to do had my father, while alive, been deeply pious, possessed by fervor or anguish of a religious nature. I then would say: It is my duty to commemorate this date according to Jewish law and custom, for such was his wish.

But though he observed tradition, my father was in no way fanatic. On the contrary, he preached an open spirit toward the world. He was a man of his time. He refused to sacrifice the present to an unforeseeable future, whatever it might be. He enjoyed simple everyday pleasures and did not consider his body an enemy. He rarely came home in the evening without bringing us special fruits and candies. Curious and tolerant, he frequented Hasidic circles because he admired their songs and stories, but refused to cloister his mind, as they did, within any given system.

My mother seemed more devout than he. It was she who brought me to heder to make me a good Jew, loving only the wisdom and truth to be drawn from the Torah. And it was she who sent me as often as possible to the Rebbe of Wizsnitz to ask his blessing or simply to expose me to his radiance.

My father's ambition was to make a man of me rather than a saint. "Your duty is to fight solitude, not to cultivate or glorify it," he used to tell me. And he would add: "God, perhaps, has need of saints; as for men, they can do without them."

He could be found more often in government offices than in the synagogue — and, sometimes, in periods of danger, even more often than at home. Every misfortune that befell our community involved him directly. There was always an impoverished, sick man who had to be sent in an emergency to a clinic in Kolozsvar or Budapest; an unfortunate shopkeeper who had to be bailed out of prison; a desperate refugee who had to be saved. Many survivors of the Polish ghettos owed their lives to him. Furnished with money and forged papers, thanks to him and his friends, they were able to flee the country for Rumania and from there to the United States or Palestine. His activities cost him three months in a Hungarian prison cell. Once released, he did not utter a word of the tortures he had undergone. On the very day of his release, he took up where he had left off.

My mother taught me love of God. As for my father, he scarcely spoke to me about the laws governing the relations between man and his creator. In our conversations, the Kaddish was never mentioned. Not even in camp. Especially not in camp.

So I do not know what he would have hoped to see me do tomorrow, the anniversary of his death. If only, in his lifetime, he had been a man intoxicated with eternity and redemption.

But that is not the problem. Even if Shlomo ben Nissel had been a faithful servant of the fierce God of Abraham, a just man, of demanding and immaculate soul, immune against weakness and doubt, even then I would not know how to interpret his death.

For I am ignorant of the essentials: what he felt, what he believed, in that final moment of his hopeless struggle, when his very being was already fading, already withdrawing toward that place where the dead are no longer tormented, where they are permitted at last to rest in peace, or in nothingness — what difference does it make?

His face swollen, frightful, bloodless, he agonized in silence. His cracked lips moved imperceptibly. I caught the sounds, but not the words of his incoherent memory. No doubt, he was carrying out his duty as father by transmitting his last wishes to me, perhaps he was also entrusting me with his final views on history, knowledge, the world's misery, his life, mine. I shall never know. I shall never know if he had the name of the Eternal on his lips to praise him — in spite of everything — or, on the contrary, because of everything, to free himself from him.

Through puffy, half-closed eyelids, he looked at me, and at times, I thought, with pity. He was leaving and it pained him to leave me behind, alone, helpless, in a world he had hoped would be different for me, for himself, for all men like him and me.

At other times, my memory rejects this image and goes its own way. I think I recognize the shadow of a smile on his lips: the restrained joy of a father who is leaving with the hope that his son, at least, will remain alive one more minute, one more day, one more week, that perhaps his son will see the liberating angel, the messenger of peace. The certitude of a father that his son will survive him.

In reality, however, I do not hesitate to believe that the truth could be entirely different. In dying, my father looked at me, and in his eyes where night was gathering, there was nothing but animal terror, the demented terror of one who, because he wished to understand too much, no longer understands anything. His gaze fixed on me, empty of meaning. I do not even know if he saw me, if it was me he saw. Perhaps he mistook me for someone else, perhaps even for the exterminating angel. I know nothing about it because it is impossible to grasp what the eyes of the dying see or do not see, to interpret the death rattle of their last breath.

I know only that that day the orphan I became did not respect tradition: I did not say Kaddish. First, because no one there would have heard and responded "Amen." Also because I did not yet know that beautiful and solemn prayer. And because I felt empty, barren: a useless object, a thing without imagination. Besides, there was nothing more to say, nothing more to hope for. To say Kaddish in that stifling barracks, in the very heart of the kingdom of death, would have been the worst of blasphemies. And I lacked even the strength to blaspheme.

Will I find the strength tomorrow? Whatever the answer, it will be wrong, at best incomplete. Nothing to do with the death of my father.

The impact of the Holocaust on believers as well as unbelievers, on Jews as well as Christians, has not yet been evaluated. Not deeply, not enough. That is no surprise. Those who lived through it, lack objectivity: They will always take the side of man confronted with the Absolute. As for the scholars and philosophers of every genre who have had the opportunity to observe the tragedy, they will — if they are capable of sincerity and humility — withdraw without daring to enter into the heart of the matter; and if they are not, well, who cares about their grandiloquent conclusions? Auschwitz, by definition, is beyond their vocabulary.

The survivors, more realistic if not more honest, are aware of the fact that God's presence at Treblinka or Maidanek — or, for that matter, his absence — poses a problem which will remain forever insoluble.

I once knew a deeply religious man who, on the Day of Atonement, in despair, took heaven to task, crying out like a wounded beast, "What do you want from me, God? What have I done to you? I want to serve you and crown you ruler of the universe, but you prevent me. I want to sing of your mercy, and you ridicule me. I want to place my faith in you, dedicate my thought to you, and you do not let me. Why? Why?"

I also knew a freethinker who, one evening, after a selection, suddenly began to pray, sobbing like a whipped child. He beat his breast, became a martyr. He had need of support, and even more, of certitude: If he suffered, it was because he had sinned; if he endured torment, it was because he had deserved it.

Loss of faith for some equaled discovery of God for others. Both answered to the same need to take a stand, the same impulse to rebel. In both cases, it was an accusation. Perhaps someday someone will explain how, on the level of man, Auschwitz was possible; but on the level of God, it will forever remain the most disturbing of mysteries.

Many years have passed since I saw my father die. I have grown up, and the candles I light several times a year in memory of departed members of my family have become more and more numerous. I should have acquired the habit, but I cannot. And each time the eighteenth day of the month of Shebat approaches, I am overcome by desolation and futility: I still do not know how to commemorate the death of my father, Shlomo ben Nissel, a death which took him as if by mistake.

Yes, a voice tells me that in reality it should suffice, as in previous years, to follow the trodden path: to study a chapter of Mishnah and to say Kaddish once again, that beautiful and moving prayer dedicated to the departed, yet in which death itself figures not at all. Why not yield? It would be in keeping with the custom of countless generations of sages and orphans. By studying the sacred texts, we offer the dead continuity if not peace. It was thus that my father commemorated the death of his father.

But that would be too easy. The Holocaust defies reference, analogy. Between the death of my father and that of his, no comparison is possible. It would be inadequate, indeed unjust, to imitate my father. I should have to invent other prayers, other acts. And I am afraid of not being capable or worthy.

All things considered, I think that tomorrow I shall go to the synagogue after all. I will light the candles, I will say Kaddish, and it will be for me a further proof of my impotence.

4

DEATH IN THE NUCLEAR AGE

By Hans J. Morgenthau

IT IS OBVIOUS that the nuclear age has radically changed man's relations to nature and to his fellowmen. It has enormously increased man's ability to use the forces of nature for his purposes and has thus concentrated unprecedented destructive powers in the hands of governments. That concentration of power has fundamentally altered the relations which have existed throughout history between government and people and among governments themselves. It has made popular revolution impossible, and it has made war an absurdity. Yet, less obvious and more important, the nuclear age has changed man's relations to himself. It has done so by giving death a new meaning.

Death is the great scandal in the experience of man; for death — as the destruction of the human person after a finite span of time — is the very negation of all man experiences as specifically human in his existence: the consciousness of himself and of his world, the remembrance of things past and the anticipation of things to come, a creativeness in thought and action which aspires to, and approximates, the eternal. Thus man has been compelled, for the sake of this existence as man, to bridge the gap between death and his specifically human attributes by transcending death. He has done so in three different ways: by making himself, within narrow limits, the master of death; by denying the reality of death through the belief in the immortality of his person; by conquering the reality of death through the immortality of the world he leaves behind.

Man can make himself the master of death by putting an end to his biological existence whenever he wishes. While he cannot live as long as he wants to, he can stop living whenever he wants to. While he cannot choose life over death when his life has reached its biological limits, he can choose death over life regardless of these limits. He can commit suicide; or he can commit what Nietzsche has called "suicide with a good conscience" by seeking out death, especially at the hand of someone else. He is capable of sacrificial death. In his self-chosen death for a particular cause, on the battlefield or elsewhere, man triumphs over death, however incompletely. He triumphs because he does not wait until his body is ready to die, but he offers his life to death when his chosen purpose demands it. Yet that triumph is incomplete because it cannot overcome the inevitability of death but only controls its coming.

Man also denies the reality of death by believing in the immortality of his person. This belief can take two different forms. It may take the form of the assumption that the finiteness of man's biological existence is but apparent and that his body will live on in another world. It can also take the form of the assumption that what is specifically human in man will survive the destruction of his body and that man's soul will live on forever, either separated from any body or reincarnated in someone else's. This belief in personal immortality, in defiance of the empirical evidence of the finiteness of man's biological existence, is of course peculiar to the religious realm. It presupposes the existence of a world which is not only inaccessible to the senses but also superior to the world of the senses in that what is truly human in man is there preserved forever.

It is a distinctive characteristic of our secular age that it has replaced the belief in the immortality of the human person with the attempt to assure the immortality of the world he leaves behind. Man can transcend the finiteness of his biological existence either in his consciousness or in objective reality by adding to that existence four different dimensions which are in one way or another independent of that finiteness. They are different dimensions of immortality. He can extend his consciousness into the past by remembering it. He can extend his consciousness into the future by anticipating it. As *homo faber,* he embeds his biological existence within technological and social artifacts which survive that existence. His imagination creates new worlds of religion, art, and reason that live after their creator.

By thus bestowing immortality upon the past, man assures himself of immortality to be granted by future generations who will remember him. As the past lives on in his historic recollection, so will he continue to live in the memory of his successors. The continuity of history gives the individual at least a chance to survive himself in the collective memory of mankind. Those who are eminent, or believe themselves to be so, aspire to posthumous fame which will enable them to live on, perhaps forever.

The ability to remember and the aspiration to be remembered call for deliberate action to assure that remembrance. The assurance of his life after death becomes one of man's main concerns here and now. Man on all levels of civilization is moved to create monuments which testify to his existence and will live after him. He founds a family and lives on in his sons, who bear his name as he bears his father's. He leaves an inheritance of visible things not to be consumed but to be preserved as tangible mementos of past generations. Over his grave he causes a monument of stone to be erected whose durability, as it were, compensates for the impermanence of what lies beneath. Or he may even refuse to accept that impermanence altogether and have his body preserved in the likeness of life. At the very least, he will have pictures made of himself to perpetuate his physical likeness.

This concern with immortality in this world manifests itself on the highest level of consciousness in the preparation of man's fame. He lives in such a way as to make sure that his fame will survive him. All of us, from the peasant and handicraft man to the founders of churches, the architects of empires, the builders of cities, the tamers of the forces of nature, seek to leave behind the works of our wills and hands to testify to our existence. *"Roma eterna,"* "the Reich of a thousand years," are but the most ambitious attempts to perpetuate man in his deeds. The tree that he has planted, the house that he has built, have been given a life likely to last longer than his own. At best, he as a person will live on in his works; at worst, he has the satisfaction of living on anonymously in what he has created.

It is, however, in the works of his imagination that man conquers the mortality of his body in the most specifically human way. The artists and poets, the philosophers and the writers, can point with different degrees of assurance to their work and say with Horace: "I have finished a monument more lasting than bronze and loftier than the Pyramids' royal pile, one that no wasting rain, no furious north wind can destroy, or the countless chain of years and the ages' flight. I shall not altogether die." In the works of his mind it is not just his physical existence, the bare fact that he once lived, that is remembered. Rather, what is remembered is the creative quality that sets him apart from all other creatures, that is peculiar to him as a man. What is remembered is not only the specifically human quality but also and most importantly the quality in which he lives on as a unique individual, the like of whom has never existed before or since. In the works of his mind, man, the creator, survives.

Yet why are those works a "monument more lasting than bronze," and why can their creator be confident that "on and on shall I grow, ever fresh with the glory of after time"? Because the man endowed with a creative mind knows himself to be a member in an unbroken chain emerging from the past and reaching into the future, which is made of the same stuff his mind is made of and, hence, is capable of participating in, and perpetuating, his mind's creation. He may be mortal, but humanity is not, and so he will be immortal in his works. This is the triumphant message of Horace.

Our life, then, receives one of its meanings from the meaning we give to death. What we make of life is shaped by what we make of death; for we live in the presence of the inevitability of death and we dedicate our lives to the proof of the proposition that death is not what it seems to be; the irrevocable end of our existence. We search for immortality, and the kind of immortality we seek determines the kind of life we lead.

The significance of the possibility of nuclear death is that it radically affects the meaning of death, of immortality, of life itself. It affects that meaning by destroying most of it. Nuclear destruction is mass destruction, both of persons and of things. It signifies the simultaneous destruction of tens of millions of people, of whole families, generations, and societies, of all the things that they have inherited and created. It signifies the total destruction of whole societies by killing their members, destroying their visible achievements, and therefore reducing the survivors to barbarism. Thus nuclear destruction destroys the meaning of death by depriving it of its individuality. It destroys the meaning of immortality by making both society and history impossible. It destroys the meaning of life by throwing life back upon itself.

Sacrificial death has meaning only as the outgrowth of an individual decision which chooses death over life. The hero who risks his life or dies for a cause is bound to be one man, an identifiable individual. There is meaning in Leonidas falling at Thermopylae, in Socrates drinking the cup of hemlock, in Jesus nailed to the cross. There can be no meaning in the slaughter of the innocent, the murder of six million Jews, the prospective nuclear destruction of, say, fifty million Americans and an equal number of Russians. There is, then, a radical difference in meaning between a man risking death by an act of will and fifty million people simultaneously reduced — by somebody switching a key thousands of miles away — to radioactive ashes, indistinguishable from the ashes of their houses, books, and animals. Horace could say, thinking of the individual soldier ready to die, "It is sweet and honorable to die for one's country." Yet Wilfred Owen, describing the effects of a gas attack in the First World War, could call Horace's famous phrase "The old Lie," and beholding a victim of modern mass destruction, could only bewail the futility of such a death and ask in despair, "Was it for this the clay grew tall? O what made fatuous sunbeams toil to break earth's sleep at all?" The death of the Horatian soldier is the assertion of man's freedom from biological necessity, a limited triumph over death. The death of Owen's soldier and of his prospective successors in the nuclear age is the negation not only of man's freedom but of his life's meaning as well.

Man gives his life and death meaning by his ability to make himself and his works remembered after his death. Patroclus dies to be avenged by Achilles. Hector dies to be mourned by Priam. Yet if Patroclus, Hector, and all those who could remember them were killed simultaneously, what would become of the meaning of Patroclus's and Hector's deaths? Their lives and deaths would lose their meaning. They would die, not like men but like beasts, killed in the mass, and what would be remembered would be the quantity of the killed — six million, twenty million, fifty million — not the quality of one man's death as over against another's.

Of their deeds, nothing would remain but the faint hope of remembrance in distant places. The very concept of fame would disappear, and the historians, the professional immortalizers, would have nothing to report. What had been preserved and created through the mind, will, and hands of man would be dissolved like man himself. Civilization itself would perish. Perhaps in some faraway place some evidence would be preserved of the perished civilization and of the men who created it. Nothing more than that would be left of the immortality man had once been able to achieve through the persistence of his fame and the permanence of his works.

And what would become of life itself? If our age had not replaced the belief in the immortality of the individual person with the immortality of humanity and its civilization, we could take the prospect of nuclear death in our stride. We could even afford to look forward to the day of the great slaughter as a day on which the preparatory and vain life on this earth would come to an end for most of us and the true, eternal life in another world begin. Yet a secular age, which has lost faith in individual immortality in another world and is aware of the impending doom of the world through which it tries to perpetuate itself here and now, is left without a remedy. Once it has become aware of its condition, it must despair. It is the saving grace of our age that it has not yet become aware of its condition.

We think and act as though the possibility of nuclear death had no bearing upon the meaning of life and death. In spite of what some of us know in our reason, we continue to think and act as though the possibility of nuclear death portended only a quantitative extension of the mass destruction of the past and not a qualitative transformation of the meaning of our existence. Thus we talk about defending the freedom of West Berlin as we used to talk about defending the freedom of the American colonies. Thus we talk about defending Western civilization against Communism as the ancient Greeks used to talk about defending their civilization against the Persians. Thus we propose to die with honor rather than to live in shame.

Yet the possibility of nuclear death, by destroying the meaning of life and death, has reduced to absurd clichés the noble words of yesterday. To defend freedom and civilization is absurd when to defend them amounts to destroying them. To die with honor is absurd if nobody is left to honor the dead. The very conceptions of honor and shame require a society that knows what honor and shame mean.

It is this contrast between our consciousness and the objective conditions in which we live, the backwardness of our consciousness in view of the possibility of nuclear death, that threatens us with the actuality of nuclear death. It would indeed be the height of thoughtless optimism to assume that something so absurd as a nuclear war cannot happen because it is so absurd. An age whose objective conditions of existence have been radically transformed by the possibility of nuclear death evades the need for a radical transformation of its thought and action by thinking and acting as though nothing of radical import had happened. This refusal to adapt thought and action to radically new conditions has spelled the doom of men and civilizations before. It is likely to do so again.

5

THE LORD WAS HIS

By Deborah Lipstadt

DEATH IS A CONCEPT that exists in the dark and distant recesses of the mind. When it rears its head it is treated in hushed and muted tones and considered to be something from which individuals — especially children — should be sheltered. It is ironic, though completely plausible, that there is an attempt to "protect" and thereby separate oneself from the reality which is death. Nothing will change that reality, and all that can be accomplished is to heighten its mysterious, incomprehensible, and frightening aspects. At the time of my father's death, in a direct encounter with the Jewish traditions of death and mourning, I found them to be the exact antithesis of the tendency to separate oneself from reality. One is gently guided through this cataclysmic period by customs and ceremonies which provide a framework for mourning, permit grief, and place the ultimate emphasis on the cyclical nature of life.

The Jewish mourning rites are a combination of various elements. The body is to be accorded the same respect that one gives to the living. It should not be mutilated, desecrated, or "improved" in any way. Even as the mourners grieve they are asked to accept God's decree. After a stipulated period of time — at the maximum one year — mourning must stop.

As a child, there were various experiences which exposed me to the concept of death and brought it into the sphere of my existence, though only to the outside parameters of that

sphere. My father was a monument dealer, and death was part
of his business. Many a family outing would be punctuated by a
stop at a cemetery in order to attend to a business detail. He
was a member of the *hevra kaddisha,* that group which is responsible for the preparation of the body prior to the funeral.
The halakhah, Jewish law, considers it a great honor and of
great importance to attend to the needs of the dead, which include cleansing the body, dressing it in the plain linen shrouds
stipulated by the Mishnah, guarding it from the time of death
until the time of burial, accompanying it to its final resting
place, and then caring for the survivors. This group of volun-
teers is called "the holy society" and not "the burial society,"
indicating the high status given it by the rabbis.

Death for my father was something that was part of the
normal life cycle. He was moved when people died, especially
those with whom he was close, but his direct connection with
the reality of death lessened the horror and terror for him.
Prior to my father's death, particularly during periods of his
illness, the possibility of his dying frightened me considerably.
Once death was imminent the reality was neither so horrifying
nor so overwhelming as I had anticipated. It brought shock, it
brought great grief, it brought loneliness, it brought anger, but
it also brought a sense of peace. The latter was prompted by
the knowledge that that which we had dreaded was finally
upon us, by a sense of relief that his suffering was soon to be
over, as well as by the type of individual my father was. He had
a unique character, a love of his fellow human being, and a
deep and abiding faith in "his" God. He related to his Master in
a very personal and private way. He trusted and accepted
God's decree. He felt himself close to his Maker, and his respect for all of God's creations was overwhelming. He was a
strictly observant Jew who loved the tradition he followed all
his life. When death came it was that tradition which guided
our actions.

Judaism has no answer for the question which haunts all
who have suffered a loss: "Why my relative and not someone
else's?" nor for the question which lies under this one: "Why *me*
— why should I have to be alone, why should I have to suffer,
why should my life be out of kilter — and not someone else?"

The first words uttered when one hears of a death are *Barukh dayan emet* — "Blessed is the truthful Judge." There are times when these words stick in the throat, as do the words of the Kaddish, which is said by the family during the year of mourning. The Kaddish, which praises God and makes no mention of the dead, is to be said only for the duration of the year, and on those occasions when memorial prayers are recited. At the end of that year we need not nor may not continue to mourn for that soul. We may remember it, miss it, long for it, but not grieve for it or for ourselves.

My father had been ill for a number of years before he passed away. The gravity of his illness forced us to confront the reality of his dying. Each bout in the hospital brought him one step closer to the end. Miraculously, when he left the hospital he regained his strength and stamina in a manner which never failed to amaze family, friends, and the medical profession.

He too had cause to reflect on his state and its implications for his future. About a year before he died he lay in his hospital bed conversing with a rabbi who had come to visit. I was standing to one side and paying only scant attention to their conversation. Suddenly I heard my father say, "I am not a wealthy man. I don't have that much to leave my children. Their greatest inheritance I have already given them." Though my eyes were still glued to the newspaper my ears were totally focused on the conversation, and I waited to hear what we had already been given. My father continued, "Love of learning, love of tradition, and respect for one's fellowman and -woman is what I have left them. It is an inheritance that I have been privileged to see them use."

Once, upon coming out of the recovery room after a serious operation, he placed a long-distance call to me to announce in a voice still heavy with sedation, "I wanted you to know that I was mentally, spiritually, and emotionally prepared for this operation and all that will follow it." Lying in bed with his skull cap on his head, he would greet all who entered the room, from the most renowned doctor to the cleaning staff, with the same warmth and respect.

I was at my father's side when he entered the coma that preceded his death. Though it was not a pretty sight, I will be eternally grateful that I was there. I saw nurses and doctors come running. I saw the orderly, who had become his friend, try to shake him awake, yelling with desperation in his voice, "Mr. Lipstadt, wake up! Please wake up!" I saw people work, I watched the hospital activate itself, and even as I watched I sensed the futility of their action. I will never have to live with the doubt that must nag so many others: "If I had been there could I have done something to save him?" Just as I remember the activity in the hospital as the medical staff tried to revive him, so too do I remember that the last thing my father did was to tell a joke. It was neither a spiritual statement nor a wise comment but a simple joke about what he was having for dinner. Five minutes after that he sat up, said, "I don't feel well," and soon became unconscious.

The doctor immediately admitted that there was extensive brain damage and that the chances for recovery were nil. I shall always be grateful for this straightforwardness. Though shaken and scared, we knew the reality of the situation, and this reality neither broke nor paralyzed us. It forced us to draw on newly discovered reservoirs of strength.

After making the necessary calls to gather the family and to say to friends, "It is not over but this is it," we turned to our rabbi. Later in the week he would guide us through the laws and customs of mourning. That night he came to the hospital and read Psalms with us. At that moment the long and very reassuring arm of tradition reached out and encircled us. It offered strength, support, and comfort during the rough road of death, funeral, mourning, and consolation. It did not answer the questions which tore at me and which tear at any individual who must confront death, but it asked that we accept that which was happening as God's just and merciful decree. I accepted, motivated by my faith and my inability to do anything else but accept.

For four days we sat and waited for the inevitable to transpire, for the end to come. This lack of activity was punctuated by frequent calls to the rabbi to check on points of halakhah and questions of "What should we do if. . . ?" The rabbi, who had been a close friend of my father, served as an authority, a reassuring figure, and one who believed but made no claims to understand God's ways. In retrospect I realize that we called him more than was necessary. The situation was not particularly complex, and we were equipped to check basic points of Jewish law on our own. However, the calls satisfied our additional needs for pastoral guidance and comforting as well as our inability to remain inactive.

Jewish law is quite precise about what is to be done with the body, who may and may not handle it (generally the body of a Jew should be handled only by Jews), how one is to act in its presence, what one is to do if present at the moment of death, and the duties and obligations incumbent on the mourner. Though each member of my family may maintain a different level of observance, throughout this period we were exactingly careful of the tradition. I frequently turned to the code of Jewish law, the Shulhan Aruk, to ascertain that I was doing all that should be done. During these emotionally chaotic times these duties and obligations provided a much needed structure for our actions.

Each member of the family who arrived at the intensive-care unit, where my father was to be for four days, came armed with a book. These were not volumes to help us pass the time but religious texts. My brother carried the Code of Jewish Law, my mother a book of Psalms which had been her rock and strength during many difficult moments, another Maurice Lamm's *The Jewish Way in Death and Mourning,* and another a volume of prayers and readings. Admittedly, our family is a bookish one with a great respect for the printed word. We instinctively turned to these volumes. They became our guides as we searched for fortitude, understanding, and faith. Observance offered a measure of strength that I never dreamed it would. We did not observe in order to be strengthened, but as we observed we were strengthened.

Death eventually came on the Sabbath. That night a few friends and neighbors gathered at the house. They made no ostensible effort to comfort us. The Mishnah notes that immediately after death and prior to interment it is impossible to console a mourner. The rabbis may have realized, as many psychologists maintain today, that it is important — if not vital — for the mourner's future mental health that at this initial period grief be worked through and anguish expressed.

On Sunday as we gathered for the funeral, we watched as

hundreds of faces, many that were known to us and many that were not, filled the room. In that crowd of seven hundred people sat many children. They had always been favorites of my father, and on the preceding day, when my father hung between life and death, they told us that during the coming week they would say special prayers for him at school. An entire class of eighth graders from a local day school was present. I looked at some of them and smiled as I recalled how they had once made elaborate plans to sneak into the hospital in order to visit their friend, Mr. Lipstadt (a few of them made it). Later when the cars lined up for the trip to the cemetery they insisted on being allowed to walk behind the hearse for a few blocks. As they did so they said Psalms. They used the tradition to pay the final respects and say good-bye to a man who had been quite special to them. I was told that they remained on the street clustered together and totally silent until long after the funeral procession was out of sight. During the following week they would appear in small groups at the house and sit quietly. Together we would recall some incident or anecdote which tied them to my father. Though retelling and recounting made our loss more vivid it also eased the pain and brought a measure of comfort.

The funeral service was unique. The rabbis chose to eulogize by telling stories about my father. He originally took ill seven years before his death. At that time he was given a number of radiation treatments over a one-week period. One of the sessions was to be on a Saturday. He inquired if it could be arranged for him to come on Friday instead of the Sabbath. Informed that Friday was the day on which terminally ill patients came for their treatments and that most outpatients found it too depressing to be present at that time, my father's answer was, "Let me try. If I get too depressed I promise to switch to Saturday." The doctor acquiesced rather unwillingly.

On that Friday my father came to the waiting room, sat down, and began to read his newspaper, and as he did so to softly hum a song. He was surrounded by people who were but shells of their former selves, many of whom were past the point where radiation would help and who seemed resigned to a certain future. He continued humming. A woman on a stretcher that was near his chair looked up and said, "That is a pretty melody." After another person commented on the song my father offered to teach it to them. As he began to teach the people near him someone cried out from the other side of the room, "I also want to learn it."

The song spread throughout the room, and soon a cacophony of voices, many of them emanating from people who could hardly talk, filled the room. When the doctor came out to call my father for his treatment he too was taught the song. As my father rose to accompany the doctor to the radiation room he turned and said, "Now that you have learned the song would you like to know the meaning of the Hebrew words which you have been singing?" Without waiting for an answer he said, "The words come from the Psalms, 'I lift up mine eyes to the mountains. From whence will my help come? My help will come from the Lord, maker of heaven and earth.'" With a slight bow and a wave of the hand as a salute to his newly formed choir, he silently turned and entered the treatment room. The silence in the waiting room was subsequently broken by the sound of one of the patients softly singing the song he had just learned.

In order to aid a struggling baker who could not get deliverymen, my father used to load up his car every Friday for a number of years and deliver cake and bread throughout the neighborhood. Many years later, when the wife of the corner newspaperman took ill and he had no one to relieve him during the eight hours he manned his newsstand, my father offered to pitch in. Each morning on the way home from synagogue services, while the newspaperman would take a short break, my father, dressed in his business suit and formal gray homburg, his face ruddy from the winter air, his red Vandyke beard trimmed to a point, and with a mischievous twinkle in his eye, would sell the morning papers to his neighbors as they passed the newsstand on their way to work. He did things such as these with a joy that comes from helping your fellowman and with a love of life that makes much of the mundane an adventure.

At the conclusion of the service, after reciting the words of the Twenty-third Psalm, "Even as I walk through the valley of the shadow of darkness I will fear no evil because you God are with me," we rose as the members of the *hevra kaddisha,* all of whom had been friends of my father, lifted the casket and carried it to the waiting hearse. At the graveside the casket was again borne by close friends and relatives. As they lowered it into the grave their faces became flushed with exertion and emotion. At no time, however, would they allow someone who had been hired for the job do the task for them. Once the casket lay in the grave, friends and relatives, young and old, worked to fill it. The impact of the fresh dirt hitting the plain pine box resounded with a harshness and clarity that made me realize that after this there was to be no more. The finality of these moments took hold as I attempted to begin to relate not to a body that lay in the ground but to a soul that was now with its God.

After a few simple prayers the immediate family performed the act of *keriah,* the tearing of one's clothes (a small tear of about an inch is made in a jacket or shirt). Though this was only a symbolic act it served as a potent physical and emotional release of sorrow and anger at precisely the needed moment. Whatever we wore during the following week was torn slightly, serving as a blatant reminder of our grief.

One should not tarry at the cemetery for too long a period of time. The soul has been entrusted to its Maker, and all that lies in the earth is the shell that housed it during its sojourn on earth. To linger at such a time would, in most cases, accent the pain and the grief. One is loath, as I was, to hurry from the cemetery. It is unhealthy to remain too long and so hard to simply turn one's back and leave. It is possible that the rabbis had this emotional dilemma in mind when they created the following custom. All those present, except the immediate family, form parallel lines a few feet apart and the mourners slowly pass through. They pause a number of times as those present say in unison, "May you be comforted among the mourners of Jerusalem and Zion." The act of leaving is done slowly. Even as one symbolically pauses, the period of mourning and the comforting that accompanies it begins. The community physically surrounds and envelops the mourner. Though they ask that God comfort you, their physical presence is a sign of their desire to ease the pain.

The meal that is eaten upon returning from the cemetery is, according to the Mishnah, to be provided by the community. The mourner should not have to eat of his own food. It is now that the community reaches out and begins to comfort. During the *shivah* period, the week following interment, the mourner is strictly forbidden to do any form of work. He may care for his own needs, but it is preferable that others do as much for him as possible. Even as we entered our home after the funeral, people from the community were waiting with food and offers of help. Neighbors arranged among themselves who would cook which meal. Others manned the phone. Still others chauffeured people to and from the airport. I shall never forget their aid and generosity and how comforting it was. On the surface they were performing the task of helping the mourner. On a deeper level, however, by busying themselves with the simplest of tasks they were dealing with the discomfort and lack of ease felt in the presence of a mourner.

It is difficult to reach out verbally to a mourner and offer words of coherent comfort. I believe that all find it difficult to offer consolation. The visitor at the house of mourning is often more ill at ease than the mourner he has come to comfort. The mourners know their position, and for them things are stark and clear-cut.

As we strictly observed the halakhah during the *shivah* period, we were constantly made aware of the significance of this time. We sat on low stools and not on comfortable chairs or sofas; we wore slippers or rubber-soled shoes and not leather ones; all symbols of vanity — jewelry, leather apparel, makeup — were proscribed for one week. Meals were prepared for us. The mirrors were covered so we would not be conscious of our looks. Those who entered the house did so silently. The door was always slightly ajar. Visitors entered, sat down, and waited for us to greet them and open the conversation. As the Mishnah explains, the mourner is to be allowed the option of remaining silent during this period. When people left they did not say good-bye but repeated the line, "May you be comforted among the mourners of Jerusalem and Zion." A candle burned for seven days and nights. We tried not to speak of mundane and everyday matters but of my father. We remembered him with both tears and laughter. We remembered the good moments and the rough ones. At times he had differed with his children and his children had differed with him. Overriding everything had been a love for one another and a shared faith in our religion and tradition. *This* was the legacy we had been left by my father. As we sat and talked with those who came to comfort, we felt that in some small measure we had to reach out and share it with them. This was a legacy of life and living, and it was incumbent on us to go on living life in the fullest way possible. These were not conscious decisions. They were extensions of all that we had seen practiced by my father. It was an inheritance given in life and not one left at death.

To ensure that we remembered the cornerstone of my father's faith, he left instructions for his funeral. They were quite basic and simple. The only one which was unique was that the service close with the singing of the *Adon Olam* according to the Portuguese melody. The *Adon Olam* is sung at the conclusion of the Sabbath service and is also part of the early-morning prayers. I thought it strange that such a proper German gentleman who believed that everything had a correct time and place should ask that the funeral close with a song.

As the cantor began to sing, others in the congregation joined in until midway through the hymn seven hundred voices were united in song. As they reached the last part of the *Adon Olam:*

וצור חבלי בעת צרה	והוא אלי וחי גואלי
מנת כוסי ביום אקרא	והוא נסי ומנוס לי
בעת אישן ואעירה	בידו אפקיד רוחי
ה׳ לי ולא אירא	ועם רוחי גויתי

He is my God and my redeemer, my rock in the time of sorrow.
On the day that I call upon him he shall be my banner and my strength.
In his hand I entrust my spirit when I sleep and when I wake.
And with that spirit I also entrust my soul, THE LORD IS MINE, I SHALL NOT FEAR.

At that moment I realized that was for us. If he was not afraid of facing death then how could the survivors be afraid?

We could be sad, we could be lonely, we could mourn, but we were not to fear.

> *Adonai lee velo erah*
> The Lord is mine I shall not fear.

6

DEATH AS HOMECOMING

By Abraham J. Heschel

OUR FIRST QUESTION is to what end and upon what right do we think about the strange and totally inaccessible subject of death? The answer is because of the supreme certainty we have about the existence of man: that it cannot endure without a sense of meaning. But existence embraces both life and death, and in a way death is the test of the meaning of life. If death is devoid of meaning, then life is absurd. Life's ultimate meaning remains obscure unless it is reflected upon in the face of death.

The fact of dying must be a major factor in our understanding of living. Yet only few of us have come face to face with death as a problem or a challenge. There is a slowness, a delay, a neglect on our part to think about it. For the subject is not exciting, but rather strange and shocking.

What characterizes modern man's attitude toward death is escapism, disregard of its harsh reality, even a tendency to obliterate grief. He is entering, however, a new age of search for meaning of existence, and all cardinal issues will have to be faced.

Death is grim, harsh, cruel, a source of infinite grief. Our first reaction is consternation. We are stunned and distraught. Slowly, our sense of dismay is followed by a sense of mystery. Suddenly, a whole life has veiled itself in secrecy. Our speech stops, our understanding fails. In the presence of death there is only silence, and a sense of awe.

Is death nothing but an obliteration, an absolute negation? The view of death is affected by our understanding of life. If life is sensed as a surprise, as a gift, defying explanation, then death ceases to be a radical, absolute negation of what life stands for. For both life and death are aspects of a greater mystery, the mystery of being, the mystery of creation. Over and above the preciousness of particular existence stands the marvel of its being related to the infinite mystery of being or creation.

Death, then, is not simply man's coming to an end. It is also entering a beginning.

There is, furthermore, the mystery of my personal existence. The problem of how and whether I am going to be after I die is profoundly related to the problem of who and how I was before I was born. The mystery of an afterlife is related to the mystery of preexistence. A soul does not grow out of nothing. Does it, then, perish and dissolve in nothing?

Human life is on its way from a great distance; it has gone through ages of experience, of growing, suffering, insight, action. We are what we are by what we come from. There is a vast continuum preceding individual existence, and it is a legitimate surmise to assume that there is a continuum following individual existence. Human living is always being under way, and death is not the final destination.

In the language of the Bible to die, to be buried, is said to be "gathered to his people" (Genesis 25:8). They "were gathered to their fathers" (Judges 2:10). "When your days are fulfilled to go to be with your fathers" (I Chronicles 17:11).

Do souls become dust? Does spirit turn to ashes? How can souls, capable of creating immortal words, immortal works of thought and art, be completely dissolved, vanish forever?

Others may counter: The belief that man may have a share in eternal life is not only beyond proof; it is even presumptuous. Who could seriously maintain that members of the human species, a class of mammals, will attain eternity? What image of humanity is presupposed by the belief in immortality?

Indeed, man's hope for eternal life presupposes that there is something about man that is worthy of eternity, that has some affinity to what is divine, that is made in the likeness of the divine.

The biblical account of creation is couched in the language of mystery. Nothing is said about the intention or the plan that preceded the creation of heaven and earth. The Bible does not begin: "And God said: Let us create heaven and earth." All we hear about is the mystery of God's creative act, and not a word about intention or meaning. The same applies to the creation of all other beings. We only hear what He does, not what He thinks. "And God said: Let there be." The creation of man, however, is preceded by a forecast. "And God said: Let us make man in our image, after our likeness." The act of man's creation is preceded by an utterance of His intention; God's knowledge of man precedes man's coming into being. God knows him before He creates him. Man's being is rooted in his being known about. It is the creation of man that opens a glimpse into the thought of God, into the meaning beyond the mystery.

"And God said: Let us make man in our image [*tzelem*], after our likeness [*demut*]. . . . And God created man in His image, in the image of God created He him" (Genesis 1:26 f.).

These words, which are repeated in the opening words of the fifth chapter of Genesis — "This is the book of the generations of man. When God created man, He made him in the likeness [*demut*] of God" — contain, according to Jewish tradition, the fundamental statement about the nature and meaning of man.

In many religions, man is regarded as an image of a god. Yet the meaning of such regard depends on the meaning of the god whom man resembles. If the god is regarded as a man magnified, if the gods are conceived of in the image of man, then such regard tells us little about the nature and destiny of man. Where God is one among many gods, where the word *divine* is used as mere hyperbolic expression, where the difference between God and man is but a difference in degree, than an expression such as "the divine image of man" is equal in meaning to the idea of the supreme in man. It is only in the light of what the biblical man thinks of God — namely, a Being who created heaven and earth, the God of justice and compassion, the master of nature and history who transcends nature and history — that the idea of man having been created in the image of God refers to the supreme mystery of man, of his nature and existence.

Image and likeness of God. What these momentous words are trying to convey has never ceased to baffle the biblical reader. In the Bible, *tzelem*, the word for "image," is nearly always used in a derogatory sense, denoting idolatrous images. (Numbers 33:52; I Samuel 6:5, 6, 11; II Kings 11:18; Ezekiel 7:20, 16:17, 23:14; II Chronicles 23:17). It is a cardinal sin to fashion an image of God. The same applies to *demut*, the word for "likeness."

"To whom will ye liken God? Or what likeness [*demut*] will ye compare to Him?" (Isaiah 40:18). "To whom will ye liken Me, and make Me equal, and compare Me, that we may be like?" (Isaiah 46:5). "For who in the skies can be compared unto the Lord, who among the sons of might can be likened unto the Lord?" (Psalms 89:7).

God is divine, and man is human. This contrast underlies all biblical thinking. God is never human, and man is never divine. "I will not execute the fierceness of Mine anger, I will not return to destroy Ephraim; for I am God and not man" (Hosea 11:9). "God is not a man, that he should lie; neither the son of man, that He should repent" (Numbers 23:19).

Thus the likeness of God means the likeness of Him who is unlike man. The likeness of God means the likeness of Him compared with whom all else is like nothing.

Indeed, the words "image and likeness of God" conceal more than they reveal. They signify something which we can neither comprehend nor verify. For what is our image? What is our likeness? Is there anything about man that may be compared with God? Our eyes do not see it; our minds cannot grasp it. Taken literally, these words are absurd, if not blasphemous. And still they hold the most important truth about the meaning of man.

Obscure as the meaning of these terms is, they undoubtedly denote something *unearthly*, something that belongs to the sphere of God. *Demut* and *tzelem* are of a higher sort of being than the things created in the six days. This, it seems, is what the verse intends to convey: Man partakes of an unearthly divine sort of being.

An idea is relevant if it serves as an answer to a question. To understand the relevance of "the divine image and likeness," we must try to ascertain the question which it comes to answer.

Paradoxically, the problem of man arises more frequently, as the problem of death than as the problem of life. It is an important fact, however, that unlike other Oriental religions, where the preoccupation with death was the central issue of religious thinking, the Bible rarely deals with death as a problem.

There is no rebellion against death, no bitterness over its sting, no preoccupation with the afterlife. In striking contrast to its two great neighboring civilizations, Egypt with its intense preoccupation with the afterlife, and Babylonia with the epic of Gilgamesh who wanders in search of immortal life, the story of the descent of Ishtar, and the legend of Nergal and Ereshkigal, the Bible is reticent in speaking about these issues. The Hebrew Bible calls for concern for the problem of living rather than the problem of dying.

Its central concern is not, as in the Gilgamesh epic, how to escape death, but rather how to sanctify life.

Man is man not because of what he has in common with the earth, but *because of what he has in common with God.* The Greek thinkers sought to understand man as *a part of the universe:* the Prophets sought to understand man as a *partner* of God.

It is a concern and a task that man has in common with God.

The intention is not to identify "the image and likeness" with a particular quality or attribute of man, such as reason, speech, power, or skill. It does not refer to something which in later systems was called "the best in man," "the divine spark," "the eternal spirit," or "the immortal element" in man. It is the whole man and every man who was made in the image and likeness of God. It is both body and soul, sage and fool, saint and sinner, man in his joy and in his grief, in his righteousness and wickedness. The image is not in man; it is man.

The basic dignity of man is not made up of his achievements, virtues, or special talents. It is inherent in his very being. The commandment "Love thy neighbor as thyself" (Leviticus 19:18) calls upon us to love not only the virtuous and the wise but also the vicious and the stupid man. The Rabbis have, indeed, interpreted the commandment to imply that even a criminal remains our neighbor (Pesahim, 75a).

The belief in the immortality of the soul seems to be derived from the belief that man is created in God's image. In Solomon's Wisdom (2:23 f.) we read: "For God created man for immortality, and made him the image of his own peculiar nature; but by the envy of the devil death entered into the world."

According to the Psalmist, however, it seems that not all people are saved from being perished. It requires an act of God's ransoming the soul from the power of Sheol for the soul to be saved.

While there is no assurance that all souls are saved from Sheol, the Psalmist does express the belief that some souls are saved.

> Like sheep they are appointed for Sheol;
> Death shall be their shepherd;
> Straight to the grave they descend,
> And their form shall waste away. . . .
> But God will ransom my soul from
> the power of Sheol,
> For He will receive me.
>
> (Psalms 49:14 – 15)

> Thou dost guide me with Thy counsel
> And afterward Thou wilt receive me
> to glory.
>
> (Psalms 73:24)

While the theme of image and likeness of God implies no dichotomy of spirit and body, another theme describing man's coming into being implies such a dichotomy.

"The Lord God formed man of the dust from the ground and breathed into his nostrils the breath of life" (Genesis 2:7). Here the distinction is sharply drawn between the aspect of man that is derived from dust and the aspect of man that goes back to God. In the spirit of these words Ecclesiastes (12:7) speaks of the eternity of the soul: "The dust returns to earth as it was, and the spirit returns to God who gave it."

"It is the spirit in a man, the breath of the Almighty, that makes him understand" (Job 32:8).

The song of Moses calls upon man: "O that . . . they would consider their latter end" (Deuteronomy 32:29). Man is made of the dust of the earth, and dying is "going the way of all the earth" (Joshua 23:14; I Kings 2:1–2). Death is "a return to the ground, for from it you were taken: For dust you are, and to dust you shall return" (Genesis 3:19). Yet the general conception is not of death as a return to dust, a dissolving into nothing.

There is a certainty of faith that the human soul will not be lost but rather be "bound in the bundle of living in the care of the Lord your God" (see I Samuel 25:29).

We are told:

Our existence carries eternity within itself. "He planted life eternal within us." Because we can do the eternal at any moment, the will of God, dying too is doing the will of God. Just as being is obedience to the Creator, so dying is returning to the Source.

Death may be a supreme spiritual act, turning oneself over to eternity: The moment of death, a moment of ecstasy. A moment of no return to vanity.

Thus afterlife is felt to be a reunion and all of life a preparation for it. The Talmud compares this world to a wedding. Said Rabbi Bunam, "If a man makes every preparation for the wedding feast but forgets to purchase a wedding ring, the marriage cannot take place." Similarly, a man may labor all his life, but if he forgets to acquire the means — to acquire the ring — the instrument of sanctifying himself to God, he will not be able to enter the life eternal.

Death may be the beginning of exaltation, an ultimate celebration, a reunion of the divine image with the divine source of being.

Dust returns to dust, while the image, the divine stake in man, is restored to the bundle of life.

Death is not sensed as a defeat but as a summation, an arrival, a conclusion.

"O God, the soul whom Thou hast placed within me is pure. Thou hast created it; Thou hast formed it; Thou hast breathed it into me. Thou preservest it within me; Thou wilt take it from me and restore it to me in the hereafter. So long as the soul is within me, I offer thanks before Thee. . . . Lord of all souls. Blessed art Thou, O Lord, who restorest the souls to the dead."

The meaning of death is in return, regardless of whether it results in a continuation of individual consciousness or in merging into a greater whole.

We are what we are by what we come from. We achieve what we do by what we hope for.

Our ultimate hope has no specific content. Our hope is God. We trust that He will not desert those who trust in Him.

> O Lord, thou hast searched me and known me!
> Thou knowest when I sit down and when I rise up;
> thou discernest my thoughts from afar.
> Thou searchest out my path and my lying down
> and art acquainted with all my ways.
> Even before a word is on my tongue,
> lo, O Lord, thou knowest it altogether.
> Thou dost beset me behind and before,
> and layest thy hand upon me.
> Such knowledge is too wonderful for me;
> it is high, I cannot attain it.
> Whither shall I go from thy Spirit?
> Or whither shall I flee from they presence?
> If I ascend to heaven, thou art there!
> If I make my bed in Sheol, thou art there!
> If I take the wings of the morning
> and dwell in the uttermost parts of the sea,
> even there thy hand shall lead me,
> and thy right hand shall hold me.
> If I say, "Let only darkness cover me,
> and the light about me be night,"
> even the darkness is not dark to thee,
> the night is bright as the day;
> for darkness is as light with thee.

(Psalms 139:1 – 12)

The ultimate hope for a life beyond the grave was not born in reflection about the soul but rather in reflection about God and what He does and means to the soul. God's being a shelter and a refuge forever held meaning to life here and now as well as to life beyond.

The meaning as well as mode of being which man hopes to

attain beyond the threshold of dying remains an impenetrable mystery. Yet it is the thought of being in God's knowing that may be both the root and the symbol of the ultimate hope.

As said above, man's being in the world is, according to the Bible, preceded by man's being known to God. Human existence follows divine anticipation. "Before I formed you in the womb I knew you" (Jeremiah 1:5). We live in the universe of His knowing.

What guides and sustains our thinking about afterlife is relatedness to God. Apart from such relatedness and trust, there is no ground for such a hope.

The real issue is whether my existence here and now is exclusively being-in-the-world or whether it is also being-in-God's-knowledge, whether being in the world is not also living in the presence of God, transcended by His knowing, escorted by His radiance.

Righteous men are regarded as living even after they die (Berakhot 18a). Just as there is a life that is really death—"The wicked are dead while they are alive" (Berakhot 18b)—so there is death that is really life.

It is the experience that those who trust in Him are not abandoned while being in the world that gives strength to the hope of not being abandoned after passing the threshold of death and leaving the world.

Daily we pray: "In Thy hand are the souls of the living and the dead as it is written 'In His hand is the soul of every living thing, and the spirit of every human being' " (Job 12:10). "Into Thy hand I commit my spirit, O Lord, faithful God Thou savest me" (Psalm 31:6).

Life after death seems to be a transposition to a unique mode of being, presumably to being in the universe of divine knowing.

The primary topic of biblical thinking is not man's knowledge of God but man's being known by God. Man's awareness of God is not awareness of God as an object of thinking but of a subject. Awareness of God is awareness of being thought of by God, of being an object of His concern, of His expectation.

Surviving after death, we hope, is surviving as a thought of God.

The question that looms in relation to my own self is: Am I worthy of surviving, of being a thought of God? What is it about myself or my existence that has affinity to eternity?

Survival beyond death carries, according to Judaism, demands and obligations during life here and now. Conditions are attached to the hope of survival.

Eternity is not an automatic consequence of sheer being, and survival is not an unconditional epilogue of living. It must be achieved, earned.

Eternal is a moment of simultaneity of the human and the divine, a moment in which God and man meet.

The religious quest is a quest of the contemporaneity of God.

Simultaneity with God is the only element of permanence in the world.

In speaking of God we have faith and a sense of presence, but no image. In speaking of life after death we have hope and a sense of trust, but no image.

Death, what follows death, is a mystery defying imagination. Facing it, our language is silence. Yet while the body descends into the grave, trust remains, hope persists and enters a simile.

Marvelous and beautiful is life in the body, but more marvelous and more beautiful is life in a word. The word is greater than world; by the word of God all was created. The Book, Scripture, is an everlasting constellation of holy words. When a good man dies, his soul becomes a word and lives in God's book.

"And many of those who sleep in the dust of the earth shall awake, some to everlasting life and some to shame and everlasting contempt" (Daniel 12:2).

The decisive message of this passage is that death is not the final act, that there will be an awakening of those who sleep in the dust.

This is the hope that in dying I become a seed and that after I decay I am born again. Must the self remain the same rather than become the seed of a new self, a new being?

We trust Him who made us what we are and will make of us what He pleases.

In spite of the excellence which the afterlife holds in store for the righteous, there is no craving for death in the history of Jewish piety. While it is true that the condition of the life beyond is eternity, it was maintained that the quality of living here and now has an excellence not given in the afterlife: freedom, serving Him in freedom. It is greater to struggle on earth than to be an angel in heaven. Earthly life, mortal life, is precisely the arena where the covenant between God and man must be fulfilled.

The love of life calls for resistance to death, resistance to the last, unconditionally.

Life here is where partnership abides between God and man. With death, man surrenders his freedom, and only God's will is done. The soul is receptive, there is no room for freedom.

Life here and now is the task. Every moment can be an achievement.

The body is not a prison, but an opportunity. Still for all its glory, life here and now is regarded as a vestibule, as preparation. Yet no one looked forward with pleasure to life after death.

Just because the afterlife is a completion, life here and now is an opportunity, and it was considered a loss to leave the realm of here and now because once the threshold is crossed the opportunity is gone.

Life is revealing of the divine, while death is concealing. To be alive is to be in the midst of the people, and we must resist being taken away from the midst of the people. But once the moment of parting comes, a benediction is uttered: Blessed be Thou, our God, King of the universe, the true Judge. Amen.

We must distinguish between being human and human being. We are born human beings. What we must acquire is being human. Being human is the essential — the decisive — achievement of a human being.

Human being finds its end in organic dissolution. But being human is not an organic substance, it is an action and a radiance of the personhood of man. The unity, the sum total of moments of personhood, is a presence that goes on in terms surpassing mere existence.

The organic process is of ambiguous significance in regard to the formation of being human. On the one hand, the organic process may compel the person to struggle for realization, but it is not always promoting it. Organic living is certainly not the total form of living.

The meaning of existence is in the sanctification of time, in lending eternity to the moments. Being human is a quest for the lasting.

Craving for God, longing for immediate perception of the divine, for emancipation from selfish desires and inclinations — such freedom can only be achieved beyond death.

It is a distortion to characterize the life of man as moving toward death. Death is the end of the road, and while moving along the long road of days and nights, we are really moving toward living, acting, achieving. Death is the end of the road, but not its meaning, not a refutation of living. That every moment of life is a step toward death is a mechanical view. Every moment of life is a new arrival, a new beginning. Those who say that we die every day, that every moment deprives us of a portion of life, look at moments as time past. Looking at moments as time present, every moment is a new arrival, a new beginning.

A man's kind deeds are used by the Lord as seeds for the planting of trees in the Garden of Eden. Each man brings about his own trees; each man creates his own Garden of Eden. In Judaism the primary dimension of existence in which meaning is both sensed and created is the dimension of deeds. Sacred acts, deeds of kindness, not only imitate the divine, they represent the divine.

Rabbi Simeon ben Yohai states: "Honor the *mitzvot*, for the *mitzvot* are my deputies, and a deputy in endowed with the authority of his principal. If you honor the *mitzvot*, it is as if you honored Me; if you dishonor them, it is as if you dishonored Me."

And the secret of spiritual living is in the sense for the ultimacy of each moment, for its sacred uniqueness, for its once-and-for-allness. It is this sense that enables us to put all our strength into sanctifying an instant by doing the holy.

Every moment is a kingdom wherein every one of us is a king by the grace of God. Does the king know what to do with his might? Our task is to design a deed, a pyramid of deeds.

There are two separate themes: death and after-death.

Death we must seek to understand in relation to life. After-death transcends that relation and must be thought of in different terms.

Death is not understood as the end of being but rather as the end of doing. As such it is a dramatic break, a radical event: cessation of doing.

We do not dwell on death. We dwell on the preciousness of every moment. Things of space vanish. Moments of time never pass away. Time is the clue to the meaning of life and death. Time lived with meaning thus is a disclosure of the eternal.

The problem is not how to mitigate the fear of death but how to conceive the meaning of death to which the meaning of life is related.

From the perspective of Love, the death of an individual is absurd and without consolation. No argument can be advanced that would offer comfort to those who mourn. The words we offer to those in mourning — "May the Lord comfort you among those who mourn for Zion and Jerusalem" — carry the hope that there is comfort for those who mourn just as there is comfort for Jerusalem when in ruin.

The thought of death is a necessary component for human existence. It enables us to be open to ultimate demands regardless of personal needs.

Anxiety about death is really an anxiety about the ultimate confrontation that follows death. In other words, it is an anxiety about the afterlife rather than about dying itself.

Life with its conflicts and contradictions, absurdities and perplexities, hurts us with a puzzlement that may lead to despair. Afterlife or the hope for the afterlife is the hope for clarification, a hope for a participation in understanding the enigma of life on earth.

One motif that is continually coming to the fore in the research dealing with attitudes toward death in terminally ill patients is "that the crisis is often not the fact of oncoming death per se, of man's insurmountable finiteness, but rather the waste of limited years, the unassayed tasks, the lacked opportunities, the talents withering in disuse, the avoidable evils which have been done. The tragedy which is underlined is that man dies prematurely and without dignity, that death has not become really his 'own'."*

There is a paradox in relation to life. To be alive is cherished as the highest value. Yet when faced with the choice of either living or committing murder, for example, we are told, Be killed rather than kill. In the course of the ages, we have been admonished to cultivate readiness to die for the sake of sanctifying the name of God.

Death is the radical refutation of man's power and a stark reminder of the necessity to relate to a meaning which lies beyond the dimension of human time. Humanity without death would be arrogance without end. Nobility has its root in humanity, and humanity derived much of its power from the thought of death.

Death refutes the deification and distorts the arrogance of man.

He is God; what he does is right, for all his ways are just; God of faithfulness and without wrong, just and right is he.

> Just art thou, O Lord, in causing death and life; thou in whose hand all living beings are kept, far be it from thee to blot out our remembrance; let thy eyes be open to us in mercy; for thine, O Lord, is mercy and forgiveness.
>
> We know, O Lord, that thy judgment is just; thou art right when thou speakest, and justified when thou givest sentence; one must not find fault with thy manner of judging. Thou art righteous, O Lord, and thy judgment is right.
>
> True and righteous Judge, blessed art thou, all whose judgments are righteous and true.
>
> The Lord gave and the Lord has taken away; blessed be the name of the Lord.
>
> Daily Prayer Book, from the Burial Service

In a broken world, cessation of living is a necessity. But someday "He will swallow up death for ever and the Lord God will wipe away tears from all faces" (Isaiah 25:8).

When Rabbi Bunam was lying on his deathbed his wife

---

*Herman Feifel, *The Meaning of Death*, New York: McGraw Hill, 1959), p. 127.

wept bitterly. When he noticed it he said to her, "Why do you cry? All my life has been given me merely that I might learn how to die."

The afterlife is thought of entirely in terms of one's trust in God.

> Even though I walk through the valley of the
> shadow of death,
> I fear no evil;
> for thou art with me;
> thy rod and thy staff,
> they comfort me.

(Psalms 23:4)

We do not know how to die in grace, because we do not know how to grow old gracefully. Growing old must be a process of cleansing the self, a way of getting ready for ultimate confrontation.

If life is a pilgrimage, death is an arrival, a celebration. The last word should be neither craving nor bitterness, but peace, gratitude.

We have been given so much. Why is the outcome of our lives, the sum of our achievements, so little?

Our embarrassment is like an abyss. Whatever we give away is so much less than what we receive. Perhaps this is the meaning of dying: to give one's whole self away.

Death is not seen as mere ruin and disaster. It is felt to be a loss of further possibilities to experience and to enhance the glory and goodness of God here and now. It is not a liquidation but a summation, the end of a prelude to a symphony of which we only have a vague inkling of hope. The prelude is infinitely rich in possibilities of either enhancing or frustrating God's patient, ongoing efforts to redeem the world.

Death is the end of what we can do in being partners to redemption. The life that follows must be earned while we are here. It does not come out of nothing; it is an ingathering, the harvest of eternal moments achieved while on earth.

Unless we cultivate sensitivity to the glory while here, unless we learn how to experience a foretaste of heaven while on earth, what can there be in store for us in life to come? The seed of life eternal is planted within us here and now. But a seed is wasted when placed on stone, into souls that die while the body is still alive.

The greatest problem is not how to continue but how to exalt our existence. The cry for a life beyond the grave is presumptuous, if there is no cry for eternal life prior to our descending to the grave. Eternity is not perpetual future but perpetual presence. He has planted in us the seed of eternal life. The world to come is not only a hereafter but also a herenow.

Our greatest problem is not how to continue but how to return. "How can I repay unto the Lord all his bountiful dealings with m?" (Psalms 116:12). When life is an answer, death is a homecoming. "Precious in the sight of the Lord is the death of his saints" (Psalms 116:14). For our greatest problem is but a resonance of God's concern: How can I repay unto man all his bountiful dealings with me? "For the mercy of God endureth forever."

This is the meaning of existence: to reconcile liberty with service, the passing with the lasting, to weave the threads of temporality into the fabric of eternity.

The deepest wisdom man can attain is to know that his destiny is to aid, to serve. We have to conquer in order to succumb; we have to acquire in order to give away; we have to triumph in order to be overwhelmed. Man has to understand in order to believe, to know in order to accept. The aspiration is to obtain; the perfection is to dispense. This is the meaning of death: the ultimate self-dedication to the divine. Death so understood will not be distorted by the craving for immortality, for this act of giving away is reciprocity on man's part for God's gift of life. For the pious man it is a privilege to die.

PART TWO

The Halakhah and Its Insights

IT IS IN THE LAW THAT Judaism comes to its most normative expression. Here then are several essays that seek to explore the meaning of several specific sections of the laws of death and mourning. The laws concerning the first day of grief, the laws of separation connected with mourning, and the laws that require and bring about a confrontation with the reality of death are examined here in turn.

Each of these essays focuses on the law, but the approach to the law varies greatly among them. For Joseph B. Soloveitchik it is the philosophical and the theological implications of the law that are the central concern. For Emanuel Feldman it is the concept of man and of human dignity reflected in the laws of mourning that is the major interest. And for Audrey Gordon it is the striking similarities between the mourning laws and the insights into grief therapy that have been obtained by the students of mental health that are the focus.

7

THE HALAKHAH OF THE FIRST DAY

By Joseph B. Soloveitchik

THERE ARE TWO DISTINCT PHASES in the process of mourning. The halakhah has meticulously insisted upon their strict separation.

The first phase begins with the death of the relative for whom one is obliged to mourn and ends with the burial. The second commences with burial and lasts seven, or with regard to some aspects, thirty days.

The first we call *aninut,* the second *avelut.* What is the halakhic and the experiential distinction between these two phases of mourning?

ANINUT

Aninut represents the spontaneous human reaction to death. It is an outcry, a shout, or a howl of grisly horror and disgust. Man responds to his defeat at the hands of death with total resignation and with an all-consuming masochistic, self-devastating black despair. Beaten by the friend, his prayers rejected, enveloped by a hideous darkness, forsaken and lonely, man begins to question his own human singular reality. Doubt develops quickly into a cruel conviction, and doubting man turns into mocking man.

At whom does man mock? At himself. He starts downgrading, denouncing himself. He dehumanizes himself. He arrives at the conclusion that man is not human, that he is just a living creature like the beasts in the field. In a word, man's initial response to death is saturated with malice and ridicule toward himself. He tells himself: If death is the final destiny of all men, if everything human terminates in the narrow, dark grave, then why be a man at all? Then why make the pretense of being the choicest of all creatures? Then why lay claim to singularity and *imago dei*? Then why be committed, why carry the human-moral load? Are we not, the mourner continues to question himself, just a band of conceited and inflated day-dreamers who somehow manage to convince themselves of some imaginary superiority over the brutes in the jungle?

The halakhah has displayed great compassion with per-plexed, suffering man firmly held in the clutches of his arch-enemy, death. The halakhah has never tried to gloss over the sorrowful, ugly spectacle of dying man. In spite of the fact that the halakhah has indomitable faith in eternal life, in immortal-ity, and in a continued transcendental existence for all human beings, it did understand, like a loving, sympathetic mother, man's fright and confusion when confronted with death. Therefore the halakhah has tolerated those "crazy," torturing thoughts and doubts. It did not command the mourner to dis-own them because they contradict the basic halakhic doctrine of man's election as the king of the universe. It permitted the mourner to have his way for a while and has ruled that the latter be relieved of all *mitzvot*.

"One whose dead relative lies before him is exempt from the recital of the Shema, and from prayer, and from *tefillin*, and from all the precepts laid down in the Torah." The Pales-tinian Talmud, quoted by Tosafot (Berakhot 17b), derives this law from the verse in Deuteronomy 16:3, "so that you may re-member the day of your departure from the land of Egypt as long as you live." The commitment accepted in Egypt is appli-cable to man who is preoccupied with life and not to one who has encountered death.

What is the reason behind this law exempting the mourner from the performance of *mitzvot*? Because our commitment to God is rooted in the awareness of human dignity and sanctity.

Once the perplexed, despairing individual begins to question whether or not such distinctiveness or choiceness exists, the whole commitment expires. Man who has faith in himself, who is aware of his charisma, was chosen and burdened with obligations and commandments. Despairing, skeptical man was not elected. How can man pray and address himself to God if he doubts his very humanity, if speech is stripped by his doubts of its human characteristics and turned into mere physical sound? How can the mourner pronounce a benediction or say "amen" if he is "speechless"? He is still capable of producing sounds, but a benediction consists of spiritual words and not just of physical sounds.

In a word, the motto of *aninut* is to be found in the old pessimistic verse in the book of Ecclesiastes: "So that man has no preeminence over the beast, for all is vanity."

AVELUT

At this point, the dialectical halakhah, which has masterfully employed both the thesis and the antithesis in her treatment of antinomies, makes an about-face. The halakhah was firmly convinced that man is free and that he is master not only of his deeds but of his emotions as well. The halakhah held the view that man's mastery of his emotional life is unqualified and that he is capable of changing thought patterns, emotional structures, and experimental motifs within an infinitesimal period of time.

Man, the halakhah maintained, does not have to wait patiently for one mood to pass and for another to emerge gradually. He disengages himself, quickly and actively, and in a wink replaces a disjunctive frame of mind with a cathartic-redemptive one. Hence, the halakhah, which showed so much tolerance for the mourner during the stage of *aninut,* and let him float with the tide of black despair, now — forcefully and with a shift of emphasis — commands him that, with interment, the first phase of grief comes abruptly to a close and a second phase — that of *avelut* — begins.

With the commencement of *avelut* the halakhah commands the mourner to undertake an heroic task: to start picking up the debris of his own shattered personality and to reestablish himself as man, restoring lost glory, dignity, and uniqueness. Instead of repeating to himself time and again that man has no preeminence over the beast and that all is vanity, he is suddenly told by the halakhah to be mindful of the antithesis: "Thou hast chosen man at the very inception and thou hast recognized him as worthy of standing before Thee."

Yes, the halakhah tells man, death is indeed something ugly and frightening, something grisly and monstrous; yes, death is trailing behind every man, trying to defeat him, his ambitions and aspirations; all that is true. Nevertheless, the halakhah adds, death must not confuse man; the latter must not plunge into total darkness because of death. On the contrary, the halakhah asserts, death gives man the opportunity to display greatness and to act heroically; to build even though he knows that he will not live to enjoy the sight of the magnificent edifice in whose construction he is engaged, to plant even though he does not expect to eat the fruit, to explore, to develop, to enrich — not himself, but coming generations.

Death teaches man to transcend his physical self and to identify with the timeless covenantal community. Death, the halakhah warns the mourner, not only does not free man from his commitment but on the contrary enhances his role as a historic being and sensitizes his moral consciousness. The day is short, the workload is heavy, the Master is strict and demanding, and the commitment therefore is great.

While before burial, in the stage of *aninut*, man mourned in total darkness and confusion, and his grief expressed itself in an act of resignation from his greatness and chosenness, after burial, in stage two, man mourns in an enlightened mood, and his grief asserts itself in the awareness of human greatness and human election.

The ceremonial turning point at which *aninut* is transformed into *avelut*, despair into intelligent sadness, and self-negation into self-affirmation, is to be found in the recital of Kaddish at the grave.

The Kaddish marks the beginning of a new phase of

courageous and heroic mourning to which the message of salvation is addressed. What is the relationship between the proclamation of the solemn doxology and burial? Through the Kaddish we hurl defiance at death and its fiendish conspiracy against man. When the mourner recites: "Glorified and sanctified be the great name . . ." he declares: No matter how powerful death is, notwithstanding the ugly end of man, however terrifying the grave is, however nonsensical and absurd everything appears, no matter how black one's despair is and how nauseating an affair life is, we declare and profess publicly and solemnly that we are not giving up, that we are not surrendering, that we will carry on the work of our ancestors as though nothing has happened, that we will not be satisfied with less than the full realization of the ultimate goal — the establishment of God's kingdom, the resurrection of the dead, and eternal life for man.

TESHUVAH

A question arises: What is the experiential substance of *avelut,* mourning, in this second phase? The latter is intrinsically an experience of *teshuvah,* of repentance. The aching heart is a contrite heart, and a contrite heart is, of course, an atoning heart. Enlightened *avelut* contains a feeling of guilt. In fact, the laws concerning the observance of *shivah* express not only a mood of grieving but also, and perhaps mainly, a mood of repenting. Quite a few of the injunctions governing the observance of *shivah,* such as the prohibitions against washing, the use of cosmetics, ointments, wearing shoes, and sex life, are reminiscent of Yom Kippur. Somehow, we arrive at a strange equation: The act of mourning equals the act of expiation. The halakhah commands the mourner to expiate his guilt with observing those prescribed rites which are also observed on the Holy Day of Atonement when man is questing for forgiveness.

What is the feeling of guilt which is implied in *avelut* and with which the halakhah is concerned?

First, death per se is a consequence of sin or human imperfection. If man were perfect, if the ultimate moral law were within his reach, if he had not fallen away from his Maker, man could combat death. As a matter of fact, we do believe that in the eschatological world where man will attain absolute perfection, death will finally be defeated. The equation of mourning and repentance is expressed in the passage in Tractate Moed Katan 15b: "A mourner is bound to overturn his couch, because Bar Kappara taught: 'God says: I have set the likeness of my image in them, and through their sins have I upset it. Let your couches be overturned on account of this.' " The passage becomes intelligible if we take into consideration that according to Talmudic and Midrashic symbolic semantics the term *mitah,* couch or bed, represents man as father and teacher, as link between past and future, both at a natural and a spiritual level. If man fails to discharge his two-fold duty, his image is tarnished and death follows. The overturned couch represents a desecrated image of man, and the mourning rites represent an act of expiation.

Second, the aspect of guilt is interwoven into the human time-consciousness. Man is a tragic as well as a comical figure in a variety of ways. However, his peculiar way of forming value judgments is the saddest of all his experiences and at the same time the most ludicrous of all his comical performances.

Man is always a latecomer as far as the formation of value judgments is concerned. His axiology or appreciation of persons, things, and events is always a product of hindsight.

In retrospection man discovers the precise value of something which, or somebody who, was but is no longer with us. This kind of tardiness in understanding and appreciating is tragic as well as comical. While the somebody was near, while I could communicate with the somebody, I was unaware of him, as if he were nobody. He comes into existence and turns into somebody important and precious at the very moment he departs from me and is lost in the mist of remoteness. Only after he has gone do I begin to ask: Who was he? What did he mean to me?

All these questions which descend in droves upon the grieving, expiating individual are extremely painful, since they are saturated with a feeling of guilt. One torturing, cruel question stands out: Why didn't I ask all these questions yesterday while the somebody was still here? The Talmud in Berakhot 42b tells a strange story: "Rav died. His disciples followed his bier. On their trip back home they stopped and ate a meal by the river Danak. When they were about to say grace they became involved in a question which they could not resolve. Whereupon Rav Addah bar Ahabah rose and made a second tear in his garment, which he had already torn once, and he said: Rav is dead and we have not learned even the rules about grace." They discovered the greatness of their master and the degree of their dependence on him on the day on which they buried him.

How sad and how ironic! They studied under him, he trained their minds, fashioned their outlook, and opened up to them new worlds of thought, and yet he remained unknown to them. They all looked upon him as "The Great Master of the Diaspora," and they all admired and revered him, and yet even they failed to see Rav's real stature and his full greatness until he had vanished from their midst.

This tragic as well as comic aspect of man is often the source of sin. The latter is precipitated by human harshness and insensitivity to the Divine Presence. Man does not feel the secret vigor, joy, and bliss that flow spontaneously from God's nearness. Man is unaware of God's working and acting through him while God uses him as the instrument of His will. Consequently, man sins; God departs and leaves man alone. Only then does lonely man comprehend the magnitude of his loss and nostalgically reach out for God. However, by the time man decides to turn to God, God is gone and man has nobody to turn to. All he finds then is an empty space and a mechanical, indifferent world. "From afar the Lord appeareth unto me" (Jeremiah 31:2). God becomes visible to man only from a distance, not when God wants to be really close to man. God allures and fascinates man from the infinite, uncharted lanes of the beyond, not while God is ready to be in immediate, intimate contact with him.

Many a time the Bible, while telling us about sin, adds significantly either "and it came to pass on the morrow" or "early next morning." Only on the morrow following the night of insensitivity and hardness to God does man begin to value divine comradeship and friendship, the happiness which he could have enjoyed if he had opened up his heart to God just a few seconds prior to God's departure.

Avelut during *shivah* or *sheloshim*, which ends on the thirtieth day after burial, is an act of atonement or expiation for both these sins, for man's insensitivity vis-à-vis God and vis-à-vis his fellowman, for not having realized who they were until they were gone.

During the mouring stage we ask the questions we should have asked before: Who was he? Whom did we lose? His image fascinates us from afar, and we ask with guilt and regret the questions that are now overdue, the questions to which only our lives can provide the answers.

8

DEATH AS ESTRANGEMENT: THE HALAKHAH OF MOURNING

By Emanuel Feldman

THE MOURNING PRACTICES of Judaism have long been the subject of discussion among students of religion. Since the Biblical-Rabbinic mourning legislation does not invest these practices with any specific rationale, nor does the Talmud express any overarching purpose which would provide a unifying frame for these apparently discrete observances, the halakhah of mourning has historically provided fertile ground for numerous investigations which, in an effort to understand its complexities, have utilized a variety of yardsticks.

Some of the early anthropologists, for example, assumed that the mourning rites were fundamentally taboo measures designed to protect the living from the feared dead. Garments were rent and sandals removed in order to prevent the dead from attaching themselves to the clothes of the living. The mourner sat on the ground and hid his face in order to confuse the returning spirits of the dead. Ashes were thrown on the face and the hair was allowed to grow long in an effort to make the mourner unrecognizable to these dreaded spirits.[1] But these scholars, in dealing with early Judaic customs, failed to take into account the fact that Biblical and Rabbinic Judaism had little patience with cults of the dead, with ancestor worship, or with rituals designed to appease the "evil" dead spirits.

Other scholars have stressed psychological, sociological, and utilitarian motifs, claiming that the mourning rites are expres-

sions of grief which should not be repressed; or that the rites
are important aids in the overcoming of grief;[2] or that they are
a necessary means for restoring the cohesion of the group
which has been profoundly shaken by death.[3]

While there is much validity to these motifs, they leave a
great deal undone and unsaid, and tend to turn the mourning
rites into a superficial textbook on group therapy. Certainly,
the mourning laws have psychological and sociological benefits.
One cannot dismiss cavalierly the impressive scholarly evidence
which has been mustered in support of Jewish mourning practices by these two disciplines. But it does an injustice to the
halakhic view of man to assume that its depths have been
plumbed simply because we are able to discover in it facets
which are congruent with current intellectual vogues.

Perhaps the search for a rationale ought to be put aside.
Instead of viewing the mourning legislation as simply a set of
laws among laws, it might prove more fruitful to view it as an
expression of a profound religious *Weltanschauung.*

This essay will investigate the mourning legislation as an
expression of the life view of Israel, and as a reflection of the
classic Judaic view of man's relationship to God, to himself, and
to death.

How should a mourner react to the fact of death? He has
now experienced the death of a close blood relative. He has felt
acutely the effects of the termination of life, and has seen the
incursion of the desacralizing elements of death into the realm
of what was once normative living. He has witnessed at close
proximity the ultimate opposite of life: He has been brushed by
the powerful nonlife, nondivine force which is death and its
accompanying *tumah,* defilement. Having known and experienced the absence of life and sanctity, he is now required by
Jewish law to crystallize this cognition into concrete observances.

The initial seven-day period immediately following death is
the most intensive period of mourning. During this time, the
following are prohibited:

1. *Cutting of the hair.* This is based on Leviticus 10:6.[4]
2. *Washing one's clothes.* This is based on II Samuel 14:2:

"And Joab sent to Tekoah and he took from there a wise woman; and he said to her, 'Do thou mourn and wear mourning clothes, and do not anoint thyself with oil, and thou shalt be as a woman mourning for her husband for many days.' " The Talmud[5] sees in the phrase "mourning clothes" a clear implication that the clothes she was bidden to wear were to be unwashed. According to one Talmudic opinion, the washing of clothes itself is not forbidden; the prohibition extends only to the wearing of newly washed garments.

3. *Anointing or washing oneself.* This too is based on the above-cited passage. Moed Katan 15b also cites Psalms 109:18, in which water is parallel to anointing with oil.[6] That washing is normally a part of anointing is indicated from Ruth 3:3, which mentions them together: "Wash and anoint thyself." According to Berakhot 2:7 in the Palestinian Talmud, they are forbidden because they give pleasure. By the same token, if the mourner is unusually dirty and washes only for the purpose of cleansing himself, but not for pleasure, this is permitted.

4. *"Use of the [conjugal] bed":* i.e., marital relations. This is derived from II Samuel 12:24, concerning David and Bathsheba. The passage implies that she was forbidden to him prior to the end of the mourning period. A mourner may not marry a wife during the mourning period, even if he does not physically consummate the marriage. Betrothal, however, is permitted.[7]

5. *Wearing of shoes,* which is derived from Ezekiel 24:17: "And thy shoes shalt thou place on thy feet," which, for the Rabbis, implies that this is permissible only to Ezekiel, because he is a priest, but is forbidden to all other mourners.[8]

6. *Working,* based on Amos 8:10: "And I will turn thy festivals into mourning." Just as a festival has in it a prohibition against work, so also is a mourner prohibited to work.

7. *Study of Scripture,* based on the same passage in Ezekiel. Moed Katan 3:5 derives this prohibition from Job 2:13, " 'And does not speak a word to him': even a word of Scripture."

8. *Sitting on a bed or couch.* This is based on II Samuel 13:31, where it is said of King David that "the King rose up and tore his clothes and lay on the ground." Additional support is in Job 2:13: "And they sat with him on the ground."[9] It is interesting that there is no requirement to sit on the ground: The

mourner may walk or stand constantly. But if he does sit, it is
not to be on a regular bed or chair, but on the ground, or on a
low stool. Related to this is the requirement to *overturn the bed,*
based on Bar Kappara's dictum:

> The Lord says, I have set the likeness of mine image on them, and
> because of their sins have I upset it; let your couches therefore be
> overturned on account thereof.

That is to say, man has distorted his divine image by sinning,
and man's sin has brought on death.[10] As an act of mourning,
he does not sleep in the normal manner.

9. *Muffling of the head* is now prescribed; that is, the
mourner must cover his head and most of his face with a ker-
chief. Known as *pri'at harosh,* this is based on Ezekiel 24:17,
which implies that a nonpriest must wrap his head. The purpose here is evidently to make the mourner look like a broken
and humbled man.[11]

10. The mourner is prohibited from giving a *greeting of
well-being.* Literally, he may not "ask one's peace," as in Genesis
24:6: "Is it peace with him? It is peace." This too is based on
Ezekiel 24:17: *he'aneh dom* — "sigh in silence." The mourner
may not give or receive greetings for the first three days of
mourning.

In addition to the above restrictions, the mourner has one
further one — and for our purposes, a very significant one. He
may not offer a sacrifice for seven days. "Rabbi Simon says, the
shlamim [sacrifice] is offered at a time when he is *shalem* [i.e.,
"complete"] and not at a time when he is on *onen.*"[12] Tosefta
Zeb. 11 states, "An *onen* is not permitted to bring a sacrifice for
the entire seven-day period."[13]

The mourning laws, it is submitted here, are a concrete
manifestation of the Judaic view of death; namely, that death
desacralizes man because it is the end of the dynamic interaction with God which can take place only in life. Death removes
man from an intimate relationship with God; he can no longer
serve Him, he can no longer perform the *mitzvot,* he no longer
possesses the *nishmat hayyim,* the breath of life, which is the dis-
tinguishing characteristic of the human being.

What of the surviving, living mourner, who alone among
the living now knows what it is to experience the end of life

and the termination of a meaningful relationship with God? In effect, the law asks the mourner to behave as if he himself were dead. He is now an incomplete person, and his daily life begins to reflect the fact of his incompleteness. His physical appearance and his body are neglected. His relationship with God is interrupted. He has no commonality or community with other men. The qualities and characteristics of a living human being are suspended. According to the Midrash, death is one of the aspects of human life which liken man to a beast.[14] In death, man has witnessed the ultimate opposite of life, of God, and of man, and he cannot now summarily leave death behind him and return quickly and easily into the land of the living. He knows now what it is to be without the breath of the God of life, and he can return to normal life and to renewed contact with the sacred only by degrees.

In a word, the mourner must now live as an alien between the two worlds of life and death, moving imperceptibly from the defiled land of *tumah* and death back toward sanctity and life.[15]

A careful examination of the specifics of the mourning legislation indicates that the laws would have the mourner react and behave in a manner consistent with that death force which he has just experienced. He has been touched by the antilife, and therefore he himself becomes less lifelike, less complete as a being. His brush with death causes him, at least for the moment, to lose his identity as a person and as a human. For just as death separates man from God, so it also separates man from the fraternity and community of other men, and separates man from his essential self, from his essence as a person. In the face of death, man as a person, as an identity, as a being, as a living creature, as the image of God, ceases to exist. The rites of mourning are a physical expression of the essential facts of death. Thus the mourner, in his conduct, is devitalized, depersonalized, deidentified in his normal relationships and connections.[16]

Therefore, he who has been involved with death and *tumah* refrains from participating in those aspects of life which express a relationship and connection with God, or fellowman, or himself. His essence as a person has been diminished, and thus he does not cut his hair, for the cutting of hair is a sign of man's concern with his person. (The Rabbis declare that an Israelite king was required to cut his hair daily, in order to maintain his dignity.[17]) The mourner allows his hair to grow unattended and uncared for; there is no concern now with his physical is-ness.

For the same reason he allows his garments to become unclean. And at the moment of death and at the burial he rends the garment he is wearing — and wears that rent garment during the mourning period. Garments and man's concern with them are manifestations of the fully living. For example, it is said of Rabbi Yohanan that he referred to his clothes as "my dignifiers."[18] That is, clothing dignifies and honors the wearer. As one who is now temporarily stripped of the dignity and honor of being a person, the mourner rends the symbol of this dignity. Further, as a manifestation of his status as a nonperson, he does not anoint or wash himself.

His is-ness as a person has been reduced, his identity as an individual has melted away, and he has no marital relations — which have the potential of creating a new life and a new identity — nor may he take a new wife.

His essence as a man has been decreased, and he walks barefoot, without shoes, in common with the beasts. Shabbat 152a reports that a Sadducee once saw Rabbi Joshua without shoes and said, "One who is dead is better off than one who goes without shoes."[19]

He has been depersonalized and may not engage in work,[20] since work sustains his life and is a manifestation of his person and of his connection with himself and with others.

He has been touched by desacralizing death and *tumah*, and he may not study Torah which is called *torat hayyim* — "the Torah of Life" (Proverbs 3:2, 3:18, 4:22, 9:11) — and which is an aspect of God and which connects man with Him and His sacredness.[21]

He has a diminished identity as a person and he does not sit, in the accepted mode of persons, on a chair or couch. He sits on the ground, in a configuration of lowness and diminution.

Because of the same consideration he refrains from sleeping in the normal mode: He "overturns the couch," and as we have noted above, the reason for this is the concept of *demut diyukni natati bakhem* — "my image have I implanted in you."[22] The image of God within man has been affected by death. That is to say, once again, that death and *tumah* have "deimagized" man who was created in the image. By virtue of his contact with death and *tumah*, the *demut diyukni* — "the form of my image" — that which makes the essential man, has been diminished. Overturning or inverting the bed during the mourning period is a symbol of this depersonalization. "Turn over the middleman (the bed on which life is conceived)," says the Talmud.[23]

For a similar reason, he does not prepare his own first meal following the burial. He has no relationship to himself, and at least at this one moment, he symbolically possesses no food. Only a fully living person prepares his own food. He may, if he desires, fast. But if he wishes to eat, the food must be prepared by others. And the menu must include such foods which remind him of the "nonperson" condition in which he finds himself.[24]

Further depersonalization takes place. The head and face are covered. In effect, the mourner says: I do not exist; I am not I; I am an alien in the land of the living.

Because he is not "I," he may not offer greetings — *sh'elat shalom* (literally, "asking of peace") — to his fellowman, nor may others offer greetings to him. He remains silent. Only a person, only an identity, can greet and be greeted in return. And *shalom* — the traditional greeting — is a symbol of community and fraternity.[25] It is significant that *shalom* is also considered to be one of the appellations of the deity, according to Shabbat 10b: "*Shalom* is the name of the Holy One, Blessed be He."[26] According to some opinions, greeting a mourner is permitted as long as the word *shalom* is not mentioned in the context of "peace unto you." According to these opinions, at least, the desacralizing aspects of death and mourning are now clearly manifested: not only is *shalom* avoided because of its connotations of peace, community, and fraternity — of which the mourner is a direct opposite; *shalom* is avoided because if its additional connotations of the sacred, from which the mourner is now estranged.[27]

In sum, the mourner is a diminished person, one who has been touched by the antilife of *tumah,* and he sits in rent garments, on the ground, without shoes, unkempt, unwashed; he engages neither in work nor in study of Torah; his head and face are covered, he greets and recognizes no one and, in turn, is greeted and recognized by no one.[28] And since he has experienced the desacralizing force of death, the *mourner may not offer up a sacrifice* for seven days.

The laws of the *onen* — the initial period of mourning immediately following death but prior to burial — offer further support for the concept of death as estranger from God. For example: The *onen* is exempt from the wearing of phylacteries; he does not recite the benediction before or after meals; he may not repeat the "amen" when he hears the benediction;[29] he does not recite the normally obligatory Shema prayer; he is exempted from all positive biblical precepts;[30] and based on Leviticus 10:19, a priest who is an *onen* is forbidden to eat of sacred food.[31]

It is precisely while the mourner is an *onen* and is existentially experiencing death at firsthand that the halakhah exempts him from performing the precepts. When death enters, man's relationship with the divine is temporarily suspended.

The rigorous halakhah of mourning thus underscores, paradoxically, the heavy Judaic stress on life, and on man's constant relationship with God, community, and himself. The dynamic interaction with God can take place only in the context of life; "the dead do not praise the Lord" (Psalms 115:); the *mitzvot* cannot be performed in a state of nonlife. Death desacralizes man and estranges him from the divine. The mourning halakhah prescribes a process of depersonalization and estrangement which is consistent with the estranging quality of death. Just as the dead are cut off from dynamic communion with God and community, so is the mourner required to behave in a similar manner — since he, alone among the living, has most intimately experienced the estrangement of death. In his conduct he refrains from participating in those aspects of life which express a relationship and connection with God, or fellowman, or with himself as a being.

NOTES

1. See A. Lods, *Israel* (New York: Alfred A. Knopf, 1962), p. 225; and R. Martin-Achard, *From Death to Life* (Edinburgh: Oliver and Boyd, 1960), pp. 25 ff.

2. Maurice Lamm, *The Jewish Way in Death and Mourning* (New York: Jonathan David, 1969), in an excellent factual presentation, occasionally reverts to "psychologizing" the rites, as on pp. 77 ff. Simon Noveck, ed., *Judaism and Psychiatry* (New York: Basic Books, 1956), pp. 105 ff., is another example of this approach, as are the two articles by I. W. Kidorf, "Jewish Tradition and the Freudian Theory of Mourning" and "The Shiva: A Form of Group Psychotherapy," *Journal of Religion and Health*, II (1962 – 63), 248 – 252, and V (1966), 43 – 47; and C. Z. Rozwaski, "On Jewish Mourning Psychology," *Judaism*, Summer 1968, pp. 335 – 345.

3. B. Malinowsky, *Magic, Science, and Religion* (Boston: Beacon Press, 1948), pp. 52 – 53.

4. Moed Katan 14b; Sem. 7; cf. Moed Katan 18a; I Sam. 4:12; Isa. 15:2, 22:12; Jer. 41:5; Mic. 1:16. Cf. J. Zandee, *Death as an Enemy According to Ancient Egyptian Conceptions* (Leiden: E. J. Brill, 1960), p. 207, for a discussion of hair as a token of mourning in Egypt. For a good summary of the mourning laws see *"Avelut,"* in *Encyclopedia Talmudit*, Vol. I (Jerusalem, 1955), pp. 26b – 36a.

5. Moed Katan 15.

6. Cf. II Sam. 14:2: ". . . mourn . . . do not anoint with oil . . ."; and Isa. 61:3: ". . . oil of joy in place of mourning. . . ."

7. Moed Katan 15b, 23a.

8. *Ibid.,* 15b, 20b; see also II Sam. 15:30.

9. See Moed Katan 15b, 15a, 21a (and 28b according to the reading of Maimonides) for the sources of these practices.

10. *Ibid.,* 15b, with the reading of Rashi; cf. J. Moed Katan 3:5; and J. Berakhot 3:1: "Bar Kappara says, A beautiful image did I have in your house, and you caused me to upset it; so also must you upset your bed." J. Berakhot 3:1 offers another reason: "Why does he sleep in an overturned bed? So that he should be awake all night and be reminded that he is a mourner." It is important to note, incidentally, that the concept of *death as affecting the divine image in man* is a key concept in the laws of mourning. The current Jewish practice of covering the mirrors in a house of mourning is a substitute for "overturning the bed." The connections between the mirror and the divine image in man are obvious.

11. See also II Sam. 15:30; Jer. 14:4; Esther 6:12.

12. Moed Katan 15a.

13. Cf. Maimonides, "Laws of Entering the Sanctuary," 2:11. For discussions on the significance of the number seven in mourning rites, see A. Kapelrud, "The Number Seven in Ugaritic Texts," *V.T.*, XVIII (1968), 495 ff., who points to seven as the number of completeness, fate, indefiniteness, danger, intensity; see also E. C. Kingsbury, "A Seven Day Ritual in the Old Babylonian Cult at Larsa," *Hebrew Union College Annual*, XXXIV (1963), 1–34; on the role of seven and other numbers in the Judaic tradition, cf. Y. Heinemann, *"Ta'amei Hamitzvot,"* *Hamador Hadati*, I, 68 f.; cf. also U. Cassuto's article in *Tarbiz*, XIII, 206–207.

14. *Genesis Rabba* 8:11.

15. This goes somewhat beyond Pedersen's view of Israelite mourning practice, in which the mourning family is aware of the discord in its life and places itself outside of normal life, as is true "in all cases where people are brought face to face with unhappiness and sorrow" which removes man from normal community. Cf. J. Pedersen, *Israel* (London: Oxford University Press, 1959), I – II, 494 ff. Pedersen, in general, is extremely sensitive to the profound issue of mourning.

16. G. von Rad refers to death as "diminished form of human existence." See his *Old Testament Theology* (New York: Harper Bros., 1960), I, 369.

17. Taanit 17a; Sanhedrin 22b. Cf. Maimonides, "Laws of Entering the Sanctuary," 1:8 – 17, where the *kohen*'s overgrown hair is a manifestation of *nivol* — "personal degradation."

18. Shabbat 13a.

19. On the subject of shoes as symbols of man's dignity, see also Shabbat 129a and Rashi *ad loc.;* Shabbat 114a; Berakhot 43b; Pesahim 112a, 113b; Yoma 78b; Ket 64b, 65b. The surviving brother who refuses to fulfill his levirate marriage obligations to the widow of his brother must undergo a *halitzah* ceremony (Deut. 25:5 – 11; Yebamot 12:1). As part of the rites, the widow "comes nigh unto him in the presence of the elders, and pulls his shoe from off his foot." In the light of the significance of the shoe, it is possible that the removal of the shoe is an attempt to strip him, at least symbolically, of his dignity as a man, since he has refused to take on the obligation of levirate marriage, i.e., to carry on the life-force of his brother *(lehakim shem)*.

20. Particularly during the first three days of mourning.

21. See also Mishnah Avot 6:7, where Torah is equated with life. Cf. Exodus Rabba 51:8: " 'Engraved — *harut* — on the tablets' (Ex. 32:16), R. Nehemiah says, Read rather *'herut'* — 'free' — free from the Angel of Death"; that is, Torah frees from death. Cf. also *ibid.*, 33.

22. Moed Katan 15b.

23. J. Moed Katan 3:5, 83a; Moed Katan 15b. On the general subject of sexual abstinence during mourning, see Norman Brown, *Life Against Death* (Middletown, Conn.: Wesleyan University Press, 1957), pp. 112 ff.; Effie Bendan, *Death Customs* (New York: Alfred A. Knopf, 1930), pp. 133, 235 f.; and H. Kelsen, *Society and Nature* (Chicago: University of Chicago Press, 1943), pp. 163 – 164: To the primitives, there is a connection between the sex act and death, and one may die during procreation unless there are proper safeguards; A. Lods, *op. cit.*, p. 271: The spirits of the act of birth should have no contact with the spirits of the dead.

That the sex act may have been the first cause of death in the world is alluded to in several Rabbinic sources, which maintain that Adam's sin was connected with the sex act. Cf. Genesis Rabba 18:6; Cantillations Rabba 4:4; Shabbat 145b; Abodah Zarah 22b; Yebamot 103b.

For more recent treatment of this subject, see Robert Gordis, "The Knowledge of Good and Evil in the Old Testament and the Dead Sea Scrolls," *JBL*, LXXVI (1957), 123 – 138; see also *American Journal of Semitic Languages*, LII (1936), 86 – 94, on this same theme.

24. Baba Batra 16b: "Why are lentils proper food for mourners? As the lentil rolls, so does mourning roll from one person to the next. As the lentil is silent (without a cleft opening), so is the mourner silent." Eggs are also mentioned as a proper mourning food, for the same reason.

25. For a contemporary discussion, within a different context, of the community aspects of the word *shalom*, see E. C. Bianchi, *Reconciliation* (New York: Sheed and Ward, 1969), p. 7.

26. See also Judg. 6:24.

27. See C. N. Denburg, ed., *Code of Hebrew Law: Yoreh De'ah* (Montreal: Jurisprudence Press, 1954), p. 300, n. 11, for an English-language discussion of greeting the mourner and *shalom*.

28. *Ibid.*, par. 390, pp. 316 ff., contains a full listing of the acts of body care prohibited to the mourner.

29. J. Berakhot 3:1.

30. Berakhot 17b; cf. *Yoreh De'ah* 341:1.

31. Horayot 12b; Maimonides, *Yad Hazakah*, "Laws of Entering the Sanctuary," 2:8; Yalkut Shimoni 533; cf. also Hos. 9:4: *k'lehem onim* —"as the bread of mourners."

9

THE PSYCHOLOGICAL WISDOM OF THE LAW

By Audrey Gordon

THE CONCEPT OF WISDOM *(hokhmah)* in the Bible is not that of
sage philosophy or metaphysical abstraction. Wisdom in the
Bible means doing what is right in each situation. It is in this
sense that the Jewish perspectives on death and the Jewish
mourning practices are "wise." They are wise because they provide a total framework within which man learns to accept
death, to mourn completely, and to live again fully.

When the family and community are faced with the prospect of the death of one of its members, Jewish law reminds us
that "a dying man is considered the same as a living man in
every respect."[1] But in American culture today, dying is treated
as if it were a separate realm of existence. America is essentially
a death-denying society; consequently we treat the dying dif-
ferently from the way we treat the living. We avoid them, or
avoid honest communication with them. We try to spare them
the problems of everyday living, and we thereby deprive them
of its joys. The dying person lives alone in an artificial environment created by those who do not wish to cope with the fact
of death and its inevitable call to every living being.

Halakhah forbids this dishonest approach. The dying person must be treated as he was always treated, as a complete
person capable of conducting his own affairs and able to enter
fully into human relations even unto death. Further, the Jewish
tradition of never leaving the bedside of the dying is of im-

mense value, not only to the dying person but also to those about to be bereaved. How helpless and how guilty we must feel when we hear of the death of a loved one, especially if no one was there to ease the fear of uncertainty and the pain of separation. All kinds of questions spring to mind from the wellsprings of guilt: "Was everything done that could have been done?" "Why didn't the doctor or nurse get there sooner?" "What could I have done to prevent this?" "Did he suffer?" "Why was he alone?" And underneath these questions lie another series of questions: "Will I suffer?" "Will I be alone?" "Will anyone care for me though I didn't care for him?" Judaism shields mourners from being overwhelmed by this kind of guilt because the community shares in the care of the dying so that they are never left alone. The community provides reassurances that everything appropriate was done. To the extent that I am a part of the communilty, part of me *was* there when he died, and so I need not fear.

The bedside vigil serves one more purpose. As death approaches, a crisis of faith occurs as the life cycle draws to an end. A personal confessional is encouraged from the dying as a rite of passage to another phase of existence. This type of confessional occurs throughout the Jewish life cycle whenever one stage has been completed. So we confess on the Day of Atonement as we end one year of life and begin another. So grooms and brides traditionally said the confessional and fasted on their wedding day, for they sensed that it marked the end of one stage in their lives and the beginning of another. The confessional on the deathbed is the recognition of the ending of one cycle and the beginning of another. This and the recitation of the Shema in the last moments before death help to affirm faith in God precisely when it is most challenged, and help the dying person focus on those most familiar rituals of his life just at the moment when he enters the most mysterious and unknowable experience of his life. This comforts him together with those who share his vigil.

The wisdom in actually observing the death is that the reality cannot then be denied. Psychiatrists know that the relatives of those missing in action or those who are lost in battle and whose bodies are never recovered have the hardest time recuperating from grief, for they have no body around which to focus and express their grief and so they are vulnerable to the temptation to deny the reality of the death. Judaism does not permit the mourner to escape the reality of death; it bids him see it, and then it leads him through a whole network of burial and mourning procedures whose purpose is to help him come to terms with it. In doing this it is in harmony with psychiatric literature, which abounds with examples of the fearful consequences of death-denial and repression of grief. The Talmudic sages centuries ago seem to have sensed the same truth that psychiatrists now articulate, which is that "the recognition of death is a necessity for continuing life, and grief is a necessary and unavoidable process in normative psychological functioning."[2]

When death occurs, Jewish law demands that immediate plans be made for burial. This is in accord with the ancient belief that it was a great dishonor and disrespect not to inter the dead. Making funeral plans serves as a necessary activity for the mourner at the beginning of the grief process. The mourner reaffirms his concern for the dead through actions which serve at the same time to overcome his wish for identification and incorporation with the lost loved one. The *onen*[3] through his actions experiences the fact that he is "not dead," not still and lifeless, as he may consciously or unconsciously feel or wish himself to be.

During this first period of grief there is an intense desire on the part of the bereaved to do whatever he can for the departed. Jewish tradition meets this need by placing the responsibility for all the funeral arrangements on the mourner, not by shielding and excusing him from these tasks. It even releases the *onen* from the obligation to perform any positive religious commandments, which on all the other days of his life are binding, so that he may devote himself instead to these burial preparations and arrangements.[4]

A funeral according to halakhah emphasizes that death is death. Realism and simplicity are the characteristics of the Jewish burial. In this respect it stands in clear contrast to the American funeral ritual, which, as Dr. Vivian Rakoff has said, "is constructed in such a way as to deny all the most obvious implications."[5] Such modern American customs as viewing the body, cosmetics, elaborate pillowed and satined coffins, and green artificial carpeting that shields the mourners from seeing the raw earth of the grave are all ways in which the culture enables us to avoid confronting the reality of death. Other associated practices such as sedating the mourners, hurrying them away from the grave, and keeping children away from the cemetery are part of the same pattern and are to be deplored. They only serve to reinforce feelings of unreality: "This isn't really happening" or "He isn't really dead." Whenever American Jews adopt such customs they cheat themselves of the valuable and healing grief work that is built into the Jewish funeral. "The disservice that the modern funeral's denial of death does to the surviving families and the rightness of expressing grief in passionate form should be publicized and explained."[6]

The simplicity of the Jewish burial averts another psychological pitfall. The religious prescription for plain, unadorned, simple coffins and for the avoidance of ostentation in the funeral itself serves as a deterrent to the excessive expenditure of family funds for irrational reasons. This expense is often the way that the family represses its guilt over past treatment of the dead or defends itself against its feelings of anger because the loved one has abandoned them. These feelings need to be worked through as a normal part of the process of grief so that later the memories of the deceased can be enjoyed without pain or avoidance. The working through of ambivalent feelings toward the dead by members of the family is extremely important in order to avoid later psychosomatic damage.[7]

I have myself conducted therapeutic interviews with such people, suffering from various forms of cancer and ulcerative colitis, in which the onset of the disease could be traced to a time shortly after a traumatic loss that had somehow not been fully faced up to and resolved. In each case the patient displayed ambivalence and unresolved grief. For example, a woman in her late sixties was admitted to the hospital with severe abdominal pains for which no physiological cause could be found. A preliminary psychiatric consultation indicated that she was severely depressed but assumed that it was simply because of her advancing age and her excessive dependency needs. But my conversation with her elicited the fact that she had not attended the funeral of her daughter who had died of cancer four years before. She had never confronted the reality of her daughter's death, and she felt somehow that God was punishing her because she had not gone to the funeral. Her pain was, in her mind, His punishment for what she had not done then. When we began the grief work and she spilled forth her guilt and her anger at her daughter for leaving her by dying, her physical symptoms began to subside and she was soon able to return home. She was still in some pain but it was now recognized for what it was, emotional pain, and therapy became helpful. Her rabbi agreed to help her continue working through her long-delayed expression of grief, and she soon recovered.

In a much more tragic case that I know, a twenty-eight-year-old man refused to permit a lifesaving operation to be performed in order to stop the spread of his cancer. His two-year-old only son had died just three months before of leukemia, and the father's grief was so overwhelming and his identification with his son was so complete that he no longer wished to live. His body heeded his mind's demands, and he died soon after.

The most striking Jewish expression of grief is the rending of garments by the mourner prior to the funeral service. The rending is an opportunity for psychological relief. It allows the mourner to give vent to his pent-up anger and anguish by means of a controlled, religiously sanctioned act of destruction.[8]

Keriah, the tearing of clothes, is a visible, dramatic symbol of the internal tearing asunder that the mourner feels in his relationship with the deceased. Even after the *shivah* is over, the garments may never be completely mended but must show the external scar of the internally healing wound. Reminders such as these constantly elicit grief reactions even as the mourner slowly begins to take up the pattern of everyday living.

Judaism opposes repression of the emotions and enjoins the mourner to express his grief and sorrow openly. In the funeral itself there are several signals for the full outpouring of grief.

The eulogy is intended to make the mourner aware of what he has lost. Traditionally, its function was to awaken tears. The familiar pattern of prayer now has a heartrending newness, as the *El male rahamim*, heard so many times before, is recited this time with the name of the dead for the first time. At the cemetery the recitation of the Kaddish stirs the memories of all who have mourned, and they join in collective sorrow together with the newly bereaved to affirm God's will and glory. The raw, gaping hole in the earth, open to receive the coffin, is symbol of the raw emptiness of the mourner at this moment of final separation. Burying the dead by actually doing some of the shoveling themselves helps the mourners and the mourning community to ease the pain of parting by performing one last act of love and concern. What more familial and poignant act is there than that of "putting to rest" as children are put to rest at night by their parents. I have seen mourners standing simply transfixed as cemetery workers callously filled in the hole until they could bear it no more and tore the shovels from their hands to finish the burial themselves.

When the burial is completed, the grief work intensifies as the focus of the community's concern shifts to the mourner. "Mourning is essentially a process of unlearning the expected presence of the deceased."[9] Returning from the cemetery the mourner finds a "meal of recuperation" waiting for him. The meal serves several purposes. First, it is a visible sign of communal solidarity, reassuring the mourner that he is not alone and that others stand ready to help him even if the one who helped him in life until now is gone. Second, it restates the theme of life and forces the mourner to recognize that his life must still go on, even though he may feel now that it too has ended with the loss of his loved one. The first mandatory meal is a resocializing and an "unlearning" experience. Until now the mourner was allowed to withdraw into his own pain and loss and identification with the deceased, but now the community reaches out to redirect him back toward the path of complete living.

With that first meal there begins the week of *shivah*, the institution through which the tradition advances the grief work for the mourner most effectively. Grief work begins with the initial release of feelings usually expressed in the recounting of the events that led up to the death, and moves from there to the recounting of the memories of the life. Edgar Jackson, writing outside the Jewish tradition, speaks unknowingly in terms that parallel the *shivah* experience when he says:

> It is important that the bereaved person have a safe framework within which he can express all the feelings that are set in motion within him by the loss of the beloved. It is also important that the means of expression meet the needs of the psyche. The ritualized religious expression does this by releasing the emotional responses that grow from group memory and group support, that justify and accept deep feelings of pain without requiring explanations, all at a level below the threshold of consciousness.[10]

The *shivah* brings the mourners together to retell and relive their experiences of the death and to share once again the memories from the past when the family circle was whole. The condolence call provides the mourner with the opportunity to tell his story many different times to many different people, each of whom is enjoined to allow the mourner to speak first so that his interests are allowed to be the focus of conversation. The visitor is not asked to say platitudes, but only to listen and by listening to enable the griever to vent his feelings. If a mourner cannot find the words with which to express his grief, then the comforter comforts him with his silence and with his shared physical presence. At a time when there are no words, the comforter should feel no need to fill the air with chatter or to divert the mourner. Silence has its own kind of eloquence, and sometimes it can be more precious than words.

Judaism recognizes that there are levels and stages of grief and so it organizes the year of mourning into three days of deep grief, seven days of mourning, thirty days of gradual readjustment, and eleven months of remembrance and healing. Thus the mourner is drawn forth from his temporary isolation to increasingly larger personal and communal responsibilities and involvements until by the end of the year he has been reintegrated into the community and his loss has been accepted, though not forgotten.

The saying of the Kaddish is such an important part of the

grieving process that women as well as men should be allowed to participate in it on an equal basis. The Women's Liberation Movement has raised our consciousnesses and made us more sensitive to the deprivation of women of religious experiences, which was unconscious and unintentional for so long. One of the first to understand it and respond to it was Henrietta Szold, the famous founder of Hadassah. Back in 1916 she wrote this letter to Hayim Peretz:

> It is impossible for me to find words in which to tell you how deeply I was touched by your offer to act as "Kaddish" for my dear mother. I cannot even thank you — it is something that goes beyond thanks. It is beautiful, what you have offered to do — I shall never forget it.
>
> You will wonder, then, that I cannot accept your offer. Perhaps it would be best for me not to try to explain to you in writing, but to wait until I see you to tell you why it is so. I know well, and appreciate what you say about the Jewish custom; and Jewish custom is very dear and sacred to me. And yet I cannot ask you to say Kaddish after my mother. The Kaddish means to me that the survivor publicly and markedly manifests his wish and intention to assume the relationship to the Jewish community which his parent had, and that so the chain of tradition remains unbroken from generation to generation, each adding its own link. You can do that for the generations of your family, I must do that for the generations of my family.
>
> I believe that the elimination of women from such duties was never intended by our law and custom — women were freed from positive duties when they could not perform them, but not when they could. It was never intended that, if they could perform them, their performance of them should not be considered as valuable and valid as when one of the male sex performed them. And of the Kaddish I feel sure this is particularly true.
>
> My mother had eight daughters and no son; and yet never did I hear a word of regret pass the lips of either my mother or my father that one of us was not a son. When my father died, my mother would not permit others to take her daughters' place in saying the Kaddish, and so I am sure I am acting in her spirit when I am moved to decline your offer. But beautiful your offer remains nevertheless, and, I repeat, I know full well that it is much more in consonance with the generally accepted Jewish tradition than is my or my family's tradition. You understand me, don't you?[11]

Henrietta Szold's affirmation of woman's rights and woman's needs in the time of mourning, written more than a half century before the current movement for woman's place of equality, should be a model for all modern Jews.

There are many customs and traditions of mourning within Judaism. Some of them are actually halakhah, others are simply customs and accretions that have attached themselves to the tradition down through the centuries. Whatever their origins, these traditions serve well the families who use them primarily as a means of expressing their loss and accepting their bereavement. The intention of all mourning practices should be the fullest possible outpouring of grief and the opportunity for the family and the community to reknit after the loss of one of its members so that they may continue to be able to love and to work. "The expression of feeling is not designed to lead to despair and to separation from the community but rather to make legitimate and more easily possible a return and a reinvestment of emotional capital in the next chapters of life."[12]

The Jewish tradition, seasoned by centuries of experience in suffering and surviving, provides this kind of a network of ways in which to affirm life in the face of death. It is a tradition that contains the wisdom that enables us to express our grief, to strengthen our family and community ties, to honor God, and to accept His will.

> On the day when death will knock at thy door
> What wilt thou offer him?
> I will set before my guest the full
>   vessel of my life.
> I will never let him go with empty hands.
>
> Rabindranath Tagore

NOTES

1. Dov Zlotnick, *The Tractate: Mourning,* Yale Judaica Series, Vol. XVII (New Haven: Yale University Press, 1966), p. 31.

2. Vivian M. Rakoff, "Psychiatric Aspects of Death in America," in Arien Mack, ed., *Death in American Experience* (New York: Schocken Books, 1974), p. 159.

3. An *onen* is a mourner from the time of the death of his relative to the time of the burial. For more on this, see "The Halakah of the First Day," page 76.

4. S. Spero, *Journey into Light* (New York: Spero Foundation, 1958), p. 22.

5. Rakoff, *op. cit.,* p. 160.

6. *Ibid.,* p. 161. I am not suggesting that when these practices are specifically requested by the family that the funeral director should ignore them, only that the family should be educated in the Jewish funeral tradition. It has been my experience that funeral directors are more than willing to conduct a funeral in the spirit and form of the Jewish tradition if the family so wishes.

7. "In acute grief the element of guilt is invariably present. This is probably due to the ambivalent quality in the love relationship where there is self-giving and self-satisfying at the same time, a craving for mutuality between the lover and the beloved, as well as the resentment at the loss of freedom that love inevitably entails. When the love object dies the feelings are set free and there is guilt" (Edgar Jackson, "Grief and Religion," in *Death in American Experience,* p. 223). The seminal article on this is still Erich Lindemann's "Symptology and Management of Acute Grief," *American Journal of Psychiatry,* CI (Sept., 1944), in which Dr. Lindemann discusses his findings in treating the bereaved survivors of the Coconut Grove fire in Boston. This study broke new ground and created interest in the scientific study of grief reactions and death attitudes.

8. Maurice Lamm, *The Jewish Way in Death and Mourning* (New York: Jonathan David, 1969), p. 38.

9. Rakoff, *op. cit.,* p. 159.

10. Jackson, *op. cit.,* p. 224.

11. "Kaddish," a letter by Henrietta Szold reprinted from *Henrietta Szold, Life and Letters,* by Marvin Lowenthal, Copyright 1942 by the Viking Press, copyright 1970 by Herman C. Emer and Harry L. Shapiro, executors for the estate of Marvin Lowenthal. Reprinted by permission of the Viking Press, Inc.

12. Jackson, *op. cit.,* p. 231.

PART THREE

Some Ultimate Questions

THESE FIVE ESSAYS all deal with the same question: how to reconcile the preciousness of life with the inevitability of death.

The question is by no means new, but it has taken on new
dimensions in our time because of the new capacities developed
by modern medicine. It is now possible to prolong life in ways
that were never contemplated before. And so we must grapple
with such questions as whether we should, and for how long,
and to what purpose, or if not, then with what safeguards and
by what right. Is there a point beyond which extraordinary
heroic measures are uncalled for, as Daniel Jeremy Silver believes? Or is life an absolute that man has no right to quantify,
as Hayim Greenberg argues? Is pain a pointless, dehumanizing
burden that diminishes the worth of life, as Abraham Kaplan
says? Or can pain be some kind of a purgative experience that
illuminates the life of man, as Hayim Greenberg suggests? Are
life and death opposites, eternal enemies, as we usually think,
or can they somehow both be contained within a greater unity,
as Milton Steinberg argues?

The conversation between C. A. Friedland and Hayim
Greenberg with which this unit ends is a conversation that goes
on simultaneously at two levels. At one level it is the encounter
of two fine minds freely associating with each other, testing
ideas and weighing possibilities, with digressions to Bialik and
Shakespeare, to Wordsworth and Werfel. But at another level
it is the conversation of two intimate friends who are sharing
with each other the little that they know about the ultimate
mystery. It is a conversation in which the dying person is the
one who wants to face the truth while the well man is the one

who wants to avoid it. They struggle back and forth, but in the end, with all their erudition, they have only their convictions, the one that there is no more than this life, the other that there is. Neither has any proof, neither has any convincing argument. They can only exchange their insights and their convictions, and one thing more — their concern for each other. In the end perhaps it is this concern, more than the cogency of their arguments or the skill of their debate — perhaps it is this concern they have for each other that has the greatest meaning.

10

THE RIGHT TO KILL?

By Hayim Greenberg

Then said Saul unto his armourbearer: "Draw thy sword and thrust me through therewith, lest these uncircumcised come and thrust me through, and abuse me." But his armourbearer would not, for he was sore afraid.
FIRST BOOK OF SAMUEL

AN OLD Syrian story relates: Man and woman (or Adam and his loyal companion Eve) were created in the fourth heaven, and there they were to live forever. But once they could not resist temptation and ate some cake, though ambrosia was their prescribed diet. The food disagreed with their celestial organisms — ambrosia, as everyone should know, is discarded through the pores of one's body a few hours after being eaten in an almost imperceptible manner — and they asked an angel to direct them to the latrine. The angel pointed to earth and said: "See that very small planet, about sixty million miles away? That is the latrine of the universe. Hasten thither." The two descended to earth and remained there forever. Since that time they eat no more ambrosia, they suffer from stomach and other ailments, some of which were cursed to remain incurable.

The Syrian story is somewhat vulgar. The people of India explain the existence of incurable diseases in a more elegant and artistic manner, and despite their innate earnestness, also more humorously. According to their story, God gave to man, immediately after his creation, a panacea for all diseases, a universal charm which assured eternal health. But man was too lazy to carry the charm with himself constantly, and he placed it on the back of the donkey he was riding. The donkey became thirsty, and a snake, the most subtle of the beasts of the field, pointed out a well. As the donkey bent down its head to drink, the snake stole the charm.

Both samples of Oriental folklore — one crude and the other more delicate — have the same motif: sickness as a perennial degradation of life. There is no escape from disease.

Is there really no escape?

Most sufferers tormented by ailments bear their allotted measure of pain and do not voluntarily renounce life. Even when they know that their disease is absolutely incurable and that their pain will daily become more unbearable, they grasp at every shadow of futile hope — mental healers, "saints," miracle workers, talismans. They await a capitulation of nature to supernature or learn to derive masochistic satisfaction and even rapture from despair itself. But in exceptional cases (heroic or cowardly) they follow the advice of Ivan Karamazov and return to God their admission cards to the sad spectacle called life. They often do so soberly, calmly, and with inner sureness, like Bacon Morris, the old English officer of whom Voltaire related the following:

"He suffered from a painful, and what appeared to be an incurable, malady. Once he came to me carrying a pocketbook and two documents. One of them, he said, was his will, the other, the text for an inscription on his tomb. In the pocketbook there was enough money to cover the funeral expenses. I have decided, he said, to try for another fourteen days what medicines and diet can do to make my life less unbearable. If these will not help, I am determined to commit suicide. You may bury me wherever you wish. The inscription on my tomb is short, only the two Latin words ascribed to Petronius — *Valete, curae.*"

The French cynic, who amused three countries with his sardonic mirth, then added: "I preach to no one but I consider it entirely correct for a man to leave his house when it no longer suits his taste." (This, by the way, is said to be a plagiarism on Frederick the Great, who declared somewhat earlier that one may not condemn a man who tires of his abode and moves to a higher story — a hint of Frederick's belief in a hereafter.)

An avenue of escape in case of unbearable and incurable

maladies thus does exist, but the number of fugitives is relatively small despite what we lately hear from doctors, especially from those who combine general medicine with psychiatry, about patients not endowed with the will-to-health who succumb to curable ailments out of a weariness of life and an unconscious refusal to be cured. However, suicides out of despair or in protest against unbearable suffering and prolonged agony still constitute a definite psychological type, who may, under certain circumstances, bring about imitation on the part of other, more normal (or abnormal) people.

Some of them are suicides only *in potentia*. There are incurables, we are told, who for some reason or other are unable to exercise the redeeming act of suicide themselves. They claim our love (or compassion) and expect us to perform for them a courageous act of mercy. Annihilation is their only hope of redemption, and they prayerfully expect us to become the executors of their suicidal wishes. Why don't we comply with their desire, with their will? Is it lack of love — of understanding love? Is it cowardice, misdirected morality? Or are we conditioned by anachronistic religious notions and taboos? That is how the matter appears to a group of our fellow citizens. You and I, and our neighbor next door, are invited by them to join an association of mercy killers. So I read in a recent advertisement carried by a number of American periodicals: "Do you believe our law should permit merciful release for incurable sufferers when they plead for it, and it is authorized by a law court after medical investigation? Then join the *Euthanasia Society of America*."

Do I believe It?

A few years ago a group of "liberal" citizens, eager to found a Euthanasia Society, honored me by asking me to endorse their undertaking. From their letter I gathered that they asked the same service of several hundred people and that they would be glad to have all of these, clergymen of all denominations, psychologists, artists, doctors, lawyers, publicists, answer in the affirmative, that mercy killing is not a crime but a positive and moral act. The men and women of that group took more than a theoretical interest in this question. They would like to see a law enacted according to which a council of doctors could decide to put an end to a human life, with the knowledge and consent of his nearest friends or relatives, when the patient is suffering from an absolutely incurable disease, his pain becomes "unbearable" and must remain so, and he himself declares his clear and conscious desire to leave the world of the living. Present laws concerning such patients are barbaric, in the opinion of that group — and apparently also of the newly founded society. We already understand, writes one of its founders, that putting to death a person who wishes to live, and whom nature endows with the resources to live, is inhumanly cruel, no matter who that person may be. But it is time for us to realize that it is equally barbarous, under certain circumstances, to force life upon a person who no longer has any use for it, who is burdened with incurable disease which daily causes him great and senseless anguish. The fact that such a person does not have the "technical courage" or the facilities to commit suicide is no proof that he does not wish to die. Such patients frequently beg their doctor, the people around, or even God, in spontaneous outbursts of prayer, to take away their life and relieve them of suffering. Why should we not fulfill their request? Why does our conscience remain untroubled when we refuse to help them for reasons of our sham humanitarianism?

The advocates of euthanasia thus ask a question to which they have a ready answer. To them it is clear that mercy killing is not only permissible, but actually a duty dictated by love for one's neighbor and genuine sympathy.

A ghastly scene emerges from my memory. A talented middle-aged Russian woman of my acquaintance who suffered from spells of hysterical elation and from subsequent attacks of what she called "oceanic depression," stopped me on Friedrichstrasse in Berlin late one winter evening and begged me to obtain for her the necessary dose of morphine which she could no longer do without. She assured me that she had already wheedled morphine from all the pharmacies of Berlin through various strategems. Now none would sell it to her, and the German doctors, as is well known, are "formalists," "legalists," "callous bureaucrats," and wouldn't do the slightest thing for you. When I refused to do her this favor and attempted to prove that I was motivated by genuine friendship, she screamed hysterically in the middle of the street: "I can't bear it any longer . . . pain all the time . . . and nothing to dull it with . . . and no hope for tomorrow. Every day is against me. . . . I can't live any longer. . . . Do me another favor then. . . . Get a knife and kill me, here, this minute. . . . I will never ask anything else of you. . . . Do it, do it, right away. . . ."

When she heard that instead I volunteered to take her home, the street resounded with the despairing tones of her cursing: "Tartar. . . . Man without heart and soul. . . . So young and already so cruel. . . . You beast of prey, sadist, Cain. . . ."

She nevertheless had enough presence of mind to be afraid of the Prussian policeman with Kaiser Wilhelm mustache and steel helmet. When she saw him crossing the street to find out what the wild scene was about, she started to run and was lost in the crowd that was streaming out of the theaters.

Five months later she died in loneliness, in a municipal hospital, after a long period of unbearable pain and convulsions.

Perhaps, I ask myself after many years, it was my duty to spare her the five months of unnecessary and senseless suffering? And if it was not *my* duty, was it not the duty of a doctor, or two, or a council of ten doctors — of society?

In 1925 a case involving mercy killing took place in Colorado. Harold Blazer, a practicing physician in a rural district of that state, chloroformed his daughter to death. His daughter had been one of the most helpless creatures in the world. Her intelligence was lower than that of any animal, in the estimation of her father. She could not speak and manifested no symptoms of any mental processes. Even the food she consumed had to be previously masticated. For years the doctor devoted all his free time to the task of keeping alive this being which could hardly be classified as human, yet was not inanimate. But as old age approached and Harold Blazer became aware that he had but a short time to live and that after his death there would be no one to look after his daughter, he determined to choloroform her to death. During the trial his attorney argued before the court that a creature such as the doctor's daughter had been could not have had a soul, and no murder was therefore committed but merely the destruction of an "object" which caused him many cares and worries for thirty years. The court acquitted Doctor Blazer.

In Gandhi's writings I find some comment on this case. He naturally does not agree with the Colorado lawyer. He felt that Dr. Blazer had murdered a *person* and not destroyed an object, for even an idiot, he holds, has a soul, and every creature which manifests even a mere physiological desire to live, no matter how undeveloped and feeble that will to live may be, is endowed with spirit. So far as the moral and legal aspects of Dr. Blazer's action are concerned, Gandhi distinguishes between two different types of judgment that should be applied to *ante-factum* and *post-factum* situations. Had the unfortunate father asked Gandhi's opinion whether he should kill his daughter out of mercy, he would have definitely told him not to, for by his intention to kill her he had manifested lack of faith in humanity and his social environment. Dr. Blazer, in the Mahatma's opinion, had no right to assume that after his death there would not be a single institution or person in the United States that would undertake to attend to the needs of his defective daughter. But once the killing had taken place, the man should not be punished legally nor greatly condemned morally. The man is not a murderer, since he committed the act out of love and sympathy and not because of selfishness or hatred. Gandhi expressed a similar opinion in another case of mercy killing that occurred in Paris when an actress killed her lover, at his own request, because he had been suffering unbearable pain from a hopelessly incurable disease. He then also maintained that there were no grounds for criminal prosecution of the actress, but that had she asked whether she had a right to execute a dear one out of love, she should have been strictly forbidden to do so. And not only she, but doctors as well should be forbidden to commit mercy killings. The Danish law which allows doctors to transform the angel of death into an angel of redemption should be done away with, he believes. (It is true that in a case involving mad dogs in an Indian town, Gandhi decided otherwise and proposed that they should be shot. For of what value is the life of a dog, a mad one at that, in a country like India where so many of the owners of the dogs do not have enough food for themselves? In this case he seems to have surrendered his belief that all living creatures — including the idiots and the mad both among people and animals — have the same right to exist for the sake of social utility, so that mad dogs should not bite and endanger the lives of sane people. However, Gandhi does not condone the idea of mercy killing where human beings are concerned.)

It is futile to discuss this question unless those who engage in the discussion have a certain area of metaphysical (or anti-metaphysical) common ground. A common language and a common point of departure are the prerequisites of any discussion. In order that a materialist or — which is perhaps more to the point — a hedonist should come to some agreement with a mystic, they would first have to reach an understanding concerning the phenomenon of suffering in general. The hedonist and materialist is by his very "constitution" unable to accept suffering. To the extent that suffering is unavoidable (or "still unavoidable," as some overoptimistic scientists would have it) he will try to adjust himself to its existence. But he will never "justify" suffering nor conceive of any inner meaning in its existence. In the ultimate analysis he may sometimes admit that the entire operation of the universe may be without logic or inherent meaning, but within the framework of that unlimited senselessness there is sense in striving to make life easier, more comfortable, more beautiful, and less painful. The religious man, on the other hand, has always sought the hidden meaning, and therefore also the justification of suffering — theodicy. Thus Rabbi Simon ben Lakish was inclined to a prophylactic interpretation of suffering, when he declared that "just as salt makes meat more tasty, so does suffering eradicate all sin from the human soul." Similarly, Rav Huna felt that suffering endows one with nothing less than life eternal. He even attempted to make a methodical classification of suffering according to its origins and nature: "When a man sees suffering coming his way, he should examine his deeds. If he has discovered no sin, he should explain his suffering on the basis of his having inadequately applied himself to the study of the Torah. If he has tried to blame it on this cause and still sees no justification for his suffering, he should then look upon it as a token of divine love for him." A similar motif is discernible in Christian literature, in the Epistles to the Hebrews, the Corinthians, and the Romans, and in the writings of St. Augustine and Thomas Aquinas.

But one need not be dogmatically religious to conceive suffering not as an accidental evil devoid of meaning, but as something inextricably bound up with the very foundations of world and existence. Friedrich von Schlegel welcomed pain and suffering: "Ailment has become the symbol of life for me. Thanks to pain I have come to see and feel the eternal contradiction through which everything comes into being and exists in this immense world of endless force and endless struggle." Pascal and Kierkegaard declared sickness to be "the natural condition of Christian man," and Novalis saw in sickness "the highest and only genuine life." It matters but little what modern psychopathologists may say about them. I am aware of all the psychological explanations that may be offered to account for their attitudes or states of mind. But when I remember Novalis's familiar claim that at the moment man begins to love sickness and suffering, there comes to him the most rapturous pleasure and he becomes imbued with the highest and most positive lust, or that "semisickness is a calamity, but total sickness is lust, the higher lust," then I am impressed that these statements are not mere spiteful *bon mots* but genuine and deeply felt experiences. One may classify them as abnormal experiences, but this clinical classification — valid and useful in its own field — can reveal nothing about their intrinsic value or their ultimate validity.

Those who have had such experiences, no matter how vague and extralogical these may be, naturally start from another angle than those who see suffering as a mere senseless accident. For some of them sickness and pain are such intense and meaningful experiences that they see in them visitations or rather visits of the holy spirit. Thus we read in the Talmud: "He who goes to visit a sick person should not sit on the bed nor on a chair nor on a bench, but should wrap himself and sit on the ground, for the Shekinah hovers over the bed of the patient." One who is capable of conceiving of the holy spirit as resting over the bed of a patient and guarding him according to its own laws, one who for one moment is capable of feeling together with Nicolai Hartmann that "great suffering reveals to us depths whose existence the uninitiated does not even suspect," does not easily find a common language with those for whom the bookkeeping of life consists of clear credit (pleasure) and clear debit (suffering), with a grand total which everyone can read, explain, and evaluate.

Everything thus depends on the point of departure — whether life can be measured in purely hedonistic terms. One may conceive of life as an enterprise, as a going concern, compare the credit and debit columns, and in a certain condition of sickness and pain logically conclude that the business is bankrupt and should be liquidated. On that basis, one may preach suicide and mercy killing, and from this point of view, be absolutely right.

But one may also conceive of life as a mission: I was *sent* here. I may not know why, wherefore, nor for how long. But my mission (or exile, as some Buddhists would say) has sense, *the* sense. This is a conception of living even against one's will, and a bookkeeper's approach is out of place in it. According to such a conception the span of one's life, whether it comes as a gift or punishment, is predetermined. Every individual life thus assumes an absolute and imperative character which neither the bearer of that life nor his enemy or friend may disrupt until it reaches its appointed epilogue. An echo of that approach one hears in an old Talmudic aphorism: "He who closes the eyes of a person in the agony of death may be compared to a murderer."

I am not going to join the Euthanasia Society. Suppose we all recognize the absolute liberty of testation, the right of every person to bring upon himself death as the deliverer from unbearable pain or hopeless disease — how could I know that the consent, the expressed desire, the prayer of the patient was genuine? I may mistake his passing mood, his violent reaction to the beginning of a new stage in the unfolding of his martyrdom, or his lyrical outburst and poetic exaggeration (hospitals are full of "poets and deceivers") for his will, for his testament. Too many of those who attempted suicide and were rescued by friends, police, or doctors, never repeated their attempts, went on living *and suffering,* and were grateful to those who thwarted their designs.

And besides, not every incurable should be given up as "hopeless." The patient may be more resourceful than medicine, and somebody else (not necessarily the *scientific* medicine man) may be required to discover and open up his untapped resources, which may not cure him, but are likely to give him a new sense of "worthwhileness." Logotherapy is as old as the human race, and the Persians of ancient days were not completely in error when they distinguished between the "herb-doctor," the "knife-doctor," and the "word-doctor." Hasidism knew something of the new life-dynamics which "the word" is capable of generating. When the famous "Yid" heard that his friend, the preacher of Kozenitz, was incurably sick, he summoned two of his pupils and instructed them: "Go to Kozenitz and sing before the Preacher." They arrived on a Friday and were invited to sing the Sabbath hymns. With every song the sick man, who had told friends that he no longer had any desire to live, felt in himself more and more strongly the awakening of a new force. He finally exclaimed: "Blessed be life! My friend, the 'Yid,' knew that I have walked in all spheres except in the sphere of song. He sent me his singers to remind me that I still have a task in my earthly life: to explore the realm of music."

11

THE RIGHT TO DIE?

By Daniel Jeremy Silver

> Of old when men lay sick and sorely tried
> The doctors gave them physic and they died.
> But here's a happier age. For now we know
> Both how to make men sick and keep them so.

I FIRST became emotionally involved with the need for a new attitude toward death years ago when, as a naval chaplain, I was quartered at a United States naval base at Yokosuka, Japan, which included a large military hospital. We were only two hours by air from the battlefields in Korea. After Marine casualties had been given emergency treatment at forward aid stations, they were airlifted to our base. One whole section of a neurosurgical ward was given over to the bodies of young men whose forebrain had been blown away by shellfire. The skills of modern surgery made it possible to stop the bleeding and close the wound, but doctors are not gods, and the control centers of the body could not be put together again. In effect, these young men were vegetables in human form. Their hearts were young. The instinct to breathe was strong. It was possible to feed them intravenously and place them on motorized cots which allowed the body fluids to move about so that these vegetables "lived" long enough to be transported back to the United States to a Veterans Administration hospital near their wives and their families; and there they could "live," the doctors told me, for a year to a year and a half before their hearts would give out or breathing would stop and death would be pronounced.

These vegetables suffered no pain, but think of the pain that was caused to their wives, children, and parents; not only the cruelty of losing a loved one in war but the cruelty of being in emotional limbo, having to visit a living corpse, having one's entire life stop for a year, a year and a half, all because medical science had kept certain organs pulsating. When I would argue with the doctors: "Why not pull the plug? Why not stop feeding this vegetable intravenously?" they answered me in terms of Navy regulations: "Our careers would be ruined if such an act were ever discovered." Others spoke of their self-definition as physicians: "We exist to heal and not to kill." One of them quoted to me that Hippocratic oath. I went back and re-searched the oath and discovered that it says that a physician may not administer a poisonous drug or give people counsel on the use of such drugs, but that the oath says nothing im-mediately relevant to the case at hand.

I do not fault the doctors; they were the heirs of a medical tradition whose standards had been built up during an age when the physician could do very little to prolong life. Doctors then lived under much suspicion, not the least of which was that they were often turned to by those who wanted poisons for all the wrong reasons. Given their history, doctors understand-ably fear for their profession if they involve themselves in ques-tionable ethical decisions which cannot be answered on purely medical and technical bases; and like us, they are products of a society which has trouble accepting death as a natural and not unwelcome part of the cycle of life. Hedonists, affluent, emo-tionally spoiled, we have forgotten or want to forget that we are born to die. We try to push off death as if death were always and ever an enemy. We fear death. We have taken it out of our homes and want to eliminate it from our lives. We've grown unaccustomed to death, and we tend to think that we must do anything and everything to keep death away from those whom we love. We've forgotten that, for many, death is a friend, a welcome visitor.

Be that as it may, the facts are that in the last quarter of a century medical technology and science have changed our capacities to deal with death in qualitative and quantitative ways, yet we still describe death in primitive and mechanistic terms. Today, when the automatic mechanisms of the body give out, we can put a body in a respirator which will force breathing. We can put a patient on a dialysis machine when his kidneys no longer function. We can put an electrical shock to the chest of the patient and restart a heart. Yet, for many, the definition of death remains no pulse, no breath, falling body temperature.

Some time ago I received a form from a member of the congregation entitled: "The Will to Live and the Right to Die." The letter is addressed "to my family, my physician, my clergyman, and my lawyer" and reads:

> If the time comes when I can no longer take part in decisions for my own future, let this statement stand as the testament of my wishes. If there is no reasonable expectation of my recovery from physical or mental disability, I request that I be allowed to die and not be kept alive by artificial means and heroic measures. Death is as much a reality as birth, growth, maturity, and old age. It is the one certainty. I do not fear death as much as I fear the indignity of deterioration dependent upon hopeless pain. I ask that drugs be mercifully administered to me for terminal suffering even if they hasten the moment of death. This request is made after careful consideration. Although this document is not legally binding, you who care for me will, I hope, feel morally bound to follow this mandate. I recognize that it places a heavy burden of responsibility upon you, and it is with the intention of sharing that responsibility and of mitigating any feelings of guilt that this statement is made.

Obviously, those who sign such a statement have had, or know about, some such experiences as the one I've described. The medical profession is well aware of this problem, but they are bound by law; they live under the fear of a malpractice suit; and it's not easy for them to come to grips with a problem which our new knowledge has placed before us.

Change can begin when we recognize that the word *death* has no specific definition. What we mean by death is what the consensus of a society, or the law of that society, describes death to be. Why is a person who stops breathing dead and a person in an irreversible coma not dead? There are attempts within and without the medical profession to develop a new definition of death, one which would take into account some of the problems raised by our medical technology. Perhaps the most hopeful undertaking is the attempt to describe death in

terms other than breathing or heartbeat. A new phrase has
emerged, *brain death,* which describes an irreversible coma,
when a person's mind is gone, after oxygen has been cut off
from the mind for a sufficient period of time so that its
capacities there have been erased. A few years ago a group called the Ad Hoc Committee of Harvard University for a Better
Definition of Brain Death defined brain death in these terms:
unresponsiveness and nonreceptivity, no reflex actions, a loss
of the body's capacity to control its motions and a flat elec-
troencephalogram indicating the absence of brain action. Obviously such a definition of death could save some families a
good deal of heartache. You and I have heard the horror
stories of those who go into an irreversible coma and because
of their youth or health have been maintained in this condition
of nonlife for six months, a year, even more. I have seen situations in which a healthy member of the family destroyed his
health in order to nurse a person who was brain-dead. I've seen
families in which the money set aside for the professional education of the young has been spent maintaining a vegetable.
There seems to be some hope that this definition of death can
become an operative one in our society.

But it's not an easy change for most people to accept. Check
your own reactions to this story which comes from an actual
case brought in the courts of Virginia some three years ago
against a group of doctors and a hospital. The charge was that
they had hastened death by removing various mechanical
means of life support. The facts were these. A laborer was hit
on the head by a heavy falling object and brought to the hospital with serious brain damage. Major surgery was attempted.
The surgery could not restore consciousness or control. The
surgeon's report indicated that the prospect of recovery was
nil. During surgery the body had been put on various support
systems including a respirator, and when it was taken to the
recovery room these systems were maintained. Some six hours
later the body was brought back to the operating room. Now
there was another patient on another bed, a patient who had
been prepared for a heart transplant. The mechanical means
of life support were stopped. The respirator was turned off.
The laborer's heart was transplanted into another body. His

family brought suit. In this case the jury accepted the testimony of Dr. Michael Sweet of Harvard University, who told the jury: "Death is a state in which the brain is dead. The rest of the body exists in order to support the brain. The brain is the individual." The hospital, the doctors, were acquitted.

What happens to your reactions when I add to this story the fact that the laborer was black and the patient to whom the heart was given was white, that the surgery was done by an all-white medical team in a white-establishment hospital? By raising such questions I suggest not only the cultural gap all of us have when it comes to accepting brain death as a functional definition, but the justice gap which makes us leery of the context in which such critical decisions will be made. If our bodies are looked on as a benevolent culture in which to keep organs alive until there is need for them in transplant surgery, what safeguards have we, if we are not of the establishment or close to the medical profession, that those who are eager for transplants will not abuse brain-death criteria in order to raid our bodies for the benefit of those whom they believe have a special right to survive? This is the gray area.

It is for reasons such as this that Judaism consistently refuses to sanction euthanasia, mercy killing, the gentle intrusion of death by some kind of positive act. In Judaism it is as much a crime to kill a fatally ill patient as it is to kill a healthy human being. There is no biblical commandment to this effect, but the Rabbis found a biblical basis for their conviction in the actions of King David. During the wars against the Philistines, a great battle took place between the Israelites under King Saul and the Philistines near Mount Gilboa. David and his troops were not involved, and afterward a young survivor appeared at David's camp and reported: "As I was moving away from the battle I chanced upon a secluded area in which I saw King Saul leaning upon his spear. He was badly wounded. He called me over saying, 'Young man, kill me. I am in terrible agony. The breath is hardly within me. I cannot survive. Put me out of my misery.' I obeyed the king." David ordered the man's execution, saying, "You have been convicted by the testimony of your own lips of having taken the life of God's anointed."

Obviously the biblical story was intended to encourage Israelites to accept the inviolate person of the king. Kings and presidents are all too frequently the object of assassination and need to be protected by a mystique as well as by a Secret Service; but no matter. The point is that the Rabbis used this story as authorization for their view that no man, under any conditions, should take the life of one who is fatally ill. They also argued that a physician who performed euthanasia was not liable before the court. He could not be put on trial. He was liable before God, but not before man. Presumably, when you make your case before God you have a far wiser court. The issue was too complex to be submitted to human judgment, but, regardless, it was a crime to take a life.

Jews lived in and among those who regularly and ruthlessly took lives. Infanticide, the exposure of unwanted or deformed youngsters, was commonplace among the Greeks. Plato insisted that the state had the right to hasten the death of the infirm or the invalid who could no longer fully contribute to its strength. He says in the *Republic* that Asklepios, the divine giver of medical knowledge, had given man only knowledge of quick and immediate cures and surgery. Asklepios did not want medicine to sustain those who could only be preserved in a state of weakness. A great society needs the strong and vibrant, who are in full control of their capacities.

Hitler drew the logical consequence of such views when he emptied the old folks' homes of Germany into the death camps, asking: "Why must Germany pay for those who never will be useful to our economy?" Similarly, Hitler went into the schools for the retarded and the nurseries which cared for mongoloids and swept these clean. After all, the state demands service from its citizens, and those who cannot serve are an unwanted burden.

The cold-blooded and calculating have always offered all manner of think-tank justification for their ruthlessness. Why sustain the aging? Of what use are they to themselves or to their families? Why sustain the malformed and retarded? How long will they survive? Who will take care of them? What kind of satisfaction can they have in their limitations? Only the religious traditions which base themselves on our Scripture have insisted on the inviolate sacredness of human life, all human life, life defined in terms of an individual soul, not in terms of social usefulness or race or class. He who destroys a single life is as if he destroys the whole world. He who saves a single life is as if he saves the whole world.

Now all this is noble, but what are we to do with the troubling problems with which our science confronts us? How can a doctor practice medicine knowing that much of what he does, if he must do everything possible to prolong life, is cruel and tragic?

There's another position in Jewish law which is based on the biblical statement that a man sentenced to death may be given certain kinds of analgesics in order to deaden his sensations so that he won't have to acknowledge the full cruelty of the hour. This commandment to mitigate pain is always in creative tension with the commandment to preserve life. The question is how to balance out their respective claims.

It seems to me that a minimal first step is to accept the new definition of death by brain death or irreversible coma. These are tests which the medical profession can easily and definitely make. If we learn to accept death in such terms, some families will be spared the guilt and confusion which overwhelm them now when a doctor says, "Should I try everything that can be done?" and the doctor will have more range for his report, "He is dead, his heart is still pumping, but life as we know it has gone." The old biblical metaphor is a good one. Death was described as the departure of the soul. I have always defined soul as personality, control, individuality, capacity, awareness. When these are gone, life has gone. Here metaphor, it seems to me, usefully goes beyond physical measurements. Children do no kindness to an elderly parent when they look at the doctor pleadingly and say, "Do everything you can do." For whom? For what? Often the answer is simply because we need to assuage our guilt.

What about the argument that we have no right to interfere in God's plan? Since God gives life, God must take life away. The only person who can logically hold this position is a Christian Scientist who has refused all medication from birth to death. The minute we go to a doctor to ask him for a cure, we interfere in God's plans. When a doctor induces a premature birth, he interferes, does he not? How much have our lives been lengthened by the immunizations, the surgery, the chemical therapies which modern medicine possesses? If we interfere on one side of the equation, certainly we can interfere on the other side.

As a second step, let us accept the fact that medical heroics are not always wise or necessary procedures. Doctors should be required to justify such heroics by positive reasons, and that justification should depend on whether or not life, in the sense of consciousness and activity, can be rekindled. It ought not to be inevitable that teams of doctors armed with all kinds of contrivances descend upon elderly patients during their last moments determined to pull them through. The question should be: What are we pulling the patient through to? It's one thing to fight for the life of a twenty-year-old whose life lies before him if there's the least chance he may regain consciousness and quite another to fight over the body of an eighty-eight-year-old whose physical strength is minimal and whose future is paralysis. These questions will not be cavalierly decided by any physician, but I would hope that my doctor would use his judgment as well as his skills if I am ever in this condition.

What am I saying? I'm saying that the miracles of modern medicine, for the first time, have made death a problem to us all. I know of many elderly who want nothing more than to be allowed to die. I don't think their suicide ought to be encouraged, but I do think that before we disturb their age with major surgery or place their life systems under mechanical support, doctors ought seriously to consider their wishes and, more often than not, allow the patient to have his way. All of us must become aware of the fact that death can no longer be described in terms of some purely instinctual pulsating organic systems, but must somehow be described in terms of mind and consciousness. The brain is the human being. We die when the brain goes. That's when the soul leaves the body. To keep a vegetable alive is to keep a vegetable alive and nothing more.

I close with a story from our Talmud. It comes from an age when people believed in the certain efficacy of prayer, when they would pray all night beside the bed of one who was mortally ill, confident that the Angel of Death could not cross the barrier of their prayers. Rabbi Joshua lay dying. His disciples had gathered in the room next door, which was both their synagogue and their school. Here they prayed hour after hour for his recovery. He couldn't die. Finally, a pious maid went into the schoolroom and stopped the disciples at their prayers. "For what are you praying? You're praying for his agony. He is with God, let him be." He died, and the Talmud praises her for this action.

12

LIFE AND DEATH AS PARTNERS

By Abraham Kaplan

For as long as there has been life, death has been the enemy. In our time medical technology has been making slow but steady progress in forestalling death. But whatever progress is made, to face death is the most universal and the most inexorable of the demands that are made on us human beings.

Because of the advances in our technology more and more human beings are dying of chronic diseases. This means that more people have time to face their own deaths and that more of us must cope with the sight of those we hold most dear slowly giving up their lives. Under these circumstances more and more of the dying communicate to us a will to die. It is time for us to face squarely the responsibilities and the moral obligations that are involved in our considering whether there is such a thing as a *right* to die. Especially must we come to terms with the guilt that we all experience in the face of death —a guilt, it may be, because we feel ourselves burdened by the dying and wish it were over and done with already, no matter how dearly we love them; and a guilt also, it may be, occasioned by the simple fact of survival: Why should others die, and we remain alive, we who have done nothing to deserve the measureless gift of life?

All these problems are conditioned in our great Judeo-Christian tradition by a fundamental principle which we know as the principle of the *sanctity of life*. Life is sacred as the locus of all other values, and therefore as in itself the supreme value. But if we are quite honest with ourselves and with one another, we must acknowledge that in few areas of the domain of value is there more hypocrisy in our society than with regard to this principle of the sanctity of life. I mean more than the appalling rise in the number of individual acts of homicide, or even the mass murders we tolerate in war. I mean also the many subtle ways in which what we profess to be the value that we place on life is not carried out in our actions. For instance, one need only consider the still shameful rate of infant mortality in the United States, or the horrifying rate of traffic fatalities, and the proliferation of many other more subtle patterns of destruction, both of ourselves and of one another. (What does it say about our civilization if we who have refused for so long to slow down on the highways in order to save lives now begin to do so in order to save gas?)

But we are hypocritical in another way as well. Though death is the enemy of life, we have contrived in our society to *glamorize* death, to paint it in the colors of life, indeed to make of it almost something more to be desired than life itself. Evelyn Waugh has written a famous satire called *The Loved One* about our patterns of denying and glossing over the bitter truths of death. I remember visiting Forest Lawn, the subject of that satire, some years ago. (That cemetery is being singled out here only as an example of many others.) As I walked around amid the manicured lawns and the splendid statuary the proposition being urged upon me there, from every side, was: "Don't grieve for the dead, they never had it so good!" There is in our time not merely a glamorization of death but also a glorification of it in ways that negate fundamental human values.

But the mere reaffirmation of the value of life will not carry us very far in dealing with our problem. Deuteronomy brings us the word of God: "Behold, I have this day set before you the way of life and the way of death. Now, therefore, choose life!" But what is a man to do when for him the way of life is blocked? The value that we place upon life, and that we enshrine in the principle of the sanctity of life, like other absolutes, conceals qualifications and circumstances and conditions which are crucial for the actualization of the value in concrete situations. One must look not to the mere continuation of life but to the *quality* of the life that is being continued.

A man is injured; he has suffered severe brain damage; he lies in a coma for hours, days, or even weeks. His life is perpetuated by the miracles of our medical technology. Yet he is no longer identifiably the person he was and who was cherished. And it may well be that there is no prospect at all of his ever returning to that identity, or even so much as ever regaining consciousness. "As though to breathe were life, to rest unburnished without use," Tennyson has the aging Ulysses say. There are deep human problems, I believe, which we must face and with which we will have to cope increasingly, in the moral principles that govern our perpetuation of life on a purely biologic level, when what we know as something distinctively human is no longer present.

In medical practice, and in the tragic experience of many families, the problem of dying becomes particularly acute when the death is a painful one. I know that there is such a thing as constructive pain. I know that without some pain the process of learning would hardly take place. But I cannot accept the doctrine that one so often hears that there is something ennobling in suffering per se. I believe pain to be a degradation of the human spirit, as Job found pain to be not the instrument for recapturing his faith but what almost cost him his faith and with it all that made life worth living.

Dante, in his poetic vision of hell in the *Inferno,* describes it as a place where there is no longer "even the hope of death"; and alas, for some death can be a hope. Nietzsche in the last century once very astutely remarked that the thought of suicide has saved many lives. The recognition, that is to say, that one can always die later gives to man the courage to face up to the agonies which he may be experiencing for a time, and which may, in time, give way to the possibility of a continuing meaningful existence. But if the agony does not give way, dying, the Roman Stoics were fond of saying, is also an act of life. How a man dies may be as much a measure of the man as how he lives. It may be, as some of the existentialists have urged in our

time, that one of the greatest tasks of the living is to learn how
to die.

Death means different things to different people, just as life
has many different meanings. To die may be perceived as
going home at last, or it may be seen as a collapsing into nothingness. It may be experienced as a triumph or it may be
experienced as a defeat. There are those for whom the whole
world comes to an end with their own existence, and others
who are so deeply identified with their fellow human beings
that their own death is only an incident in the ongoing events
that have meaning and value far beyond the boundaries of
their own lives.

To die in a manner that is worthy of a human being is to
die with a sense of one's own identity as the human being that
he is; as the locus of all the human values which intersect,
which come to a meeting point, in his being; as an embodiment
of human dignity. It is well to remember that even though the
victims of inhumanity have been robbed of their lives, no one
can rob a man of his humanity, of his soul, if he holds it fast.
We must all die, to be sure; with regard to that there is no
choice. But choice remains, if we choose to allow it to remain,
as to the manner of dying. I think, for example, of some
documents which were found in the Warsaw ghetto after the
end of World War II. These documents recorded the meetings
in which the decision to revolt was arrived at in the Warsaw
ghetto. The decision was not made with any expectation that a
handful of men would be able to fight off the Wehrmacht, and
certainly not with any notion that a miracle would be brought
about and that God would see to it that the Nazis were destroyed. The decision to fight was much more earthbound, but
at the same time it expressed the limitless reaches of the human
spirit even in the face of death. What they decided was how to
die — like men, not like rats caught in a sewer. They faced the
question not of whether to die — life was no longer among the
options open to these good men and women. The choice they
made was of how to die, the choice between dying like the great
and noble human spirits that they were or of allowing themselves to be reduced to the level of bestiality of those who were
destroying them. They faced the question in moral terms, in

human terms, and they died as befits human beings.

The central issue in our relationship to the dying is to know that the dying patient is not "the lung cancer on the fourth floor" but a person, a person whom you know and who knows you and who perhaps is reaching out to you as all that remains to him of a human contact. For you to abandon him is understandable, for you also have your own fears. Neither the physician nor the philosopher nor the clergyman nor the relative is exempt from the common fate of mankind as though from some Olympus we looked down on suffering mortals and decided what we might do to alleviate their lot. Our own mortality is very much with us when we look at them. But it is our task to counter that tendency to depersonalization and avoidance, to maintain our humanity and the humanity of the patient as long as that is at all possible. For we the living are dehumanized if we dehumanize the dying. Precisely when they stand in greatest need of human closeness and warmth, our own fears and our own guilts turn us away from them. We imagine that we can continue to deceive them about their own condition and that we are doing so as an act of kindness to them. It is that in part, of course, but it is also an act of kindness to ourselves and an act of cowardice. It may be that a man has a right to know when his life is drawing to a close, and a right also to share with us that knowledge of those last hours of his, so that he can die at peace with himself and with others, not isolated and abandoned precisely by those who mean the most to him. There are some very simple, and I find, still very moving lines by Emily Dickinson beginning with "My life closed twice before its close" and ending with "parting is all we know of heaven and all we need of hell." For indeed, the taste of hell comes in that other closing which is no part of dying, except as we permit it to be a part, when we turn our backs upon the dying, perhaps for their sakes and perhaps for ours, perhaps to deny the inevitability of our own death, and perhaps somehow to free ourselves of the burden of helplessness in the face of the imminent death of someone in our care.

I believe that we ought to recognize another principle, coordinate with the principle of the sanctity of life, and that is the principle of the *acceptance of death*. This certainly does not mean giving up, surrendering to the enemy, or betraying the values for which life is the precondition. It simply means recognizing death as the inevitable accompaniment and culmination of life.

This is the great wisdom of the Jewish faith and the Christian faith and every mature faith which holds on at one and the same time to two complementary affirmations — that life is good and that death is inevitable. It is the faith of Job, who was able to declare: "God gave, and God has taken away. Blessed be the name of God." When Job said that, he had come to an acceptance of the ills that all flesh is heir to, and he was able to experience life as a blessing, even with those ills.

At the end of Ingmar Bergman's deeply religious picture *The Seventh Seal,* the knight, his squire, his wife, and those accompanying him are caught in the castle by Death, who finally comes to claim them as his own. What do human beings do when Death appears? They plead and argue, until at last he calls out "silence!" Then the squire, who throughout the picture has shown man's capacity to see himself and his fate with realism, rejoins, "I will be silent — but under protest." These last words convey, it seems to me, the way in which we ought to relate to death. We ought to protest it every single step of the way — but we ought to know that it is going to end in silence.

The image of life that I like to have is of an unaging psyche with an aging soma. The soma will age as part of natural processes which only fantasies can deny. But there is something ageless in the psyche — in our occasional glimpses of truth, in our visions of beauty, in the depths of our commitments to moral ideas, and in the deep fulfillments of our giving and receiving love. In all these things is something by virtue of which man is not merely an animal caught up in the process of generation and decay. He is also the locus of something eternal. And it is this which is the most significant part of what makes us human beings.

To die as a human being requires a sense of legacy, a sense of continuity in time beyond the boundaries of the soma, a faith in the future. A man's capacity to face up to his death is proportional to his capacity to face up to life. In the words of that wonderful Yiddish proverb, *"Der vos lebt un takhlis shtarbt un vidui"* — "He who lives without purpose must die without confession." When a life has been fulfilled, then death presents itself as a closure in which dignity still remains. But if life has been empty and unfulfilled, then not all the ministrations of all the healing arts can transform it into anything other than a scene of pathos, in place of the tragedy it might have risen to.

No one can summarize his life in a single memorable sentence, yet somehow that retrospective view puts things in a better perspective than a man can have while he is caught up in all his doings. I love that patient who was able to say at the end: "It's been a good life, and the last year of it was the best." I should suppose that such a person probably said that every year, and that he said of every hour *This* is the best hour. To live so deeply, with such a sense of fulfillment in the present moment, is indeed to know the life eternal while alive.

There is a legend in the Jewish tradition of a great sage named Rabbi Meir who had two sons whom he loved dearly. On a day when he was away from home, the two of them died suddenly within the same hour. His wife Beruriah tenderly laid them out in another room and covered them. When he returned she waited until the Sabbath was over, for the Sabbath cannot be spoiled for death, only for the sake of saving life. Then when the Sabbath had come to its close, she broke the news to him this way: She said to him, "Many years ago a stranger passed this way and left in my safekeeping two precious jewels. He has been gone so long that I have come to feel that these jewels are my own. Now today unexpectedly he reappeared and demanded that I give him back what is his. Must I, indeed, give them up?" Rabbi Meir said to her, "How can you doubt where the course of virtue lies?" She took him by the hand to the other room, threw back the sheet, and said, "There lie the jewels." I love that story because its wisdom is for all of us. There must surely come a time to each one of us when the jewels that have been put into our safekeeping are called back from us. And nothing is more characteristically human than for us to feel, "Not yet! Now is not the time!"

The ability to accept death depends upon its being a death in good time. It is in good time when it is in the fullness of years, and the fullness of years is not. something to be measured only in their number but also in their quality. Years are full when their days and their hours are full. Years are full when they are rich in fulfillments. So long as a person can feel that each year of his life is the best, that each day is better than the days that have gone before, and that in this hour he knows the joy as well as the pain and the burden of being human, his life is being fulfilled. Otherwise death comes as a cheat and is met with bitterness. For how can one be ready to accept death if he has not yet accepted life or if life has not yet accepted him?

There is a story in Scripture of the prophet Balaam, who was called upon to curse the Israelites, and who instead could only bless them, even expressing for himself the hope, "May I die the death of the righteous; may my end be like theirs." He looked down upon their encampment and said, "How beautiful are your tents, O Jacob, how goodly your tabernacles." To be able to look upon human habitations and to see them as beautiful even though they are tents, even though they will be folded up and the people will pass on, is to live, it seems to me, the life of the righteous, and to be able then to die, to come to an end, as the righteous do. We might wish that we could live in stone buildings, but all of us must live in tents. To be able to see that and yet to see the beauty in the tents is the beginning of wisdom.

I know no faith that loves life, that celebrates life, that values life as much as does the faith of Israel. But I know no faith that sees life as realistically, that sees death as part of life, that sees the sanctity of life overflowing into the acceptance of death, that sees both life and death as coming from the same source and therefore both as blessed, as does the faith of Israel.

The psalmist could envision both life and death when he said: "My cup runneth over." He could see beyond the horizon of this life when he declared in simple trust: "May goodness and mercy follow me all the days of my life," and then: "May I dwell in the house of the Lord forever."

13

TO HOLD WITH OPEN ARMS

By Milton Steinberg

IT IS A SOUND CONVENTION which requires that a sermon begin with a text — some verse from Scripture, or from Rabbinic literature, which summarizes the theme. But it is well to understand that a text is, after all, only the soul-experience of some man boiled down to the size of an epigram. At some time in the past a prophet or a saint met God, wrestled with good or evil, tasted of life and found it bitter or sweet, contemplated death, and then distilled the adventure into a single line, for those that would come after him. That is a text.

But it is not only the great, the saints, the prophets, and the heroes who contemplate God, life, and death. We, too, the plainer folk of the world, live, love, laugh, and suffer, and by no means always on the surface. We, too, catch glimpses of eternity and the things that people do. Not only of Moses, but of us, too, it may be said, as Lowell put it:

> Daily with souls that cringe and plot
> We Sinais climb and know it not.

There are texts in us, too, in our commonplace experiences, if only we are wise enough to discern them.

One such experience, a *textual* experience, so to speak, fell to my lot not so long ago. There was nothing dramatic about its setting nor unusual in its circumstances. And yet to me it was a moment of discovery, almost of revelation.

Let me recount it very briefly, as befits a text. After a long illness, I was permitted for the first time to step out-of-doors. And as I crossed the threshold sunlight greeted me. This is my experience — all there is to it. And yet, so long as I live, I shall never forget that moment. It was mid-January — a time of cold and storm up North, but in Texas, where I happened to be, a season much like our spring. The sky overhead was very blue, very clear, and very, very high. Not, I thought, the *shamayim*, heaven, but *shemei shamayim*, a heaven of heavens. A faint wind blew from off the western plains, cool and yet somehow tinged with warmth — like a dry, chilled wine. And everywhere in the firmament above me, in the great vault between the earth and sky, on the pavements, the buildings — the golden glow of the sunlight. It touched me, too, with friendship, with warmth, with blessing. And as I basked in its glory there ran through my mind those wonderful words of the prophet about the sun which someday shall rise with healing on its wings.

In that instant I looked about me to see whether anyone else showed on his face the joy, almost the beatitude, I felt. But no, there they walked — men and women and children, in the glory of the golden flood, and so far as I could detect, there was none to give it heed. And then I remembered how often I, too, had been indifferent to sunlight, how often, preoccupied with petty and sometimes mean concerns, I had disregarded it. And I said to myself, How precious is the sunlight but alas, how careless of it are men. How precious — how careless. This has been a refrain sounding in me ever since.

It rang in my spirit when I entered my own home again after months of absence; when I heard from a nearby room the excited voices of my children at play; when I looked once more on the dear faces of some of my friends; when I was able for the first time to speak again from my pulpit in the name of our faith and tradition, to join in worship of the God who gives us so much of which we are so careless.

And a resolution crystallized within me. I said to myself that at the very first opportunity I would speak of this. I knew full well that it is a commonplace truth, that there is nothing clever about my private rediscovery of it, nothing ingenious about my way of putting it. But I was not interested in being original or

clever or ingenious. I wanted only to remind my listeners, as I
was reminded, to spend life wisely, not to squander it.

I wanted to say to the husbands and wives who love one
another: "How precious is your lot in that it is one of love. Do
not be, even for a moment, casual with your good fortune.
Love one another while yet you may."

And to parents: "How precious is the gift of your children.
Never, never be too busy for the wonder and miracle of them.
They will be grown up soon enough and grown away, too."

We human beings, we frail reeds who are yet, as Pascal said,
thinking reeds, *feeling* reeds, how precious are our endowments
— minds to know, eyes to see, ears to listen, hearts to stir with
pity, and to dream of justice and of a perfected world. How
often are we indifferent to all these!

And we who are Jews and Americans, heirs of two great
traditions, how fortunate our lot in both, and how blind we are
to our double good fortune.

This is what struggled in me for utterance — as it struggled
in Edna St. Vincent Millay when she cried out:

O world I cannot hold thee close enough.

I want to urge myself and all others to hold the world tight
— to embrace life with all our hearts and all our souls and all
our might. For it is precious, ineffably precious, and we are
careless, wantonly careless of it.

And yet, when I first resolved to express all this, I knew
that it was only a half-truth.

Could I have retained the sunlight no matter how hard I
tried? Could I have prevented the sun from setting? Could I
have kept even my own eyes from becoming satiated and bored
with the glory of the day? That moment had to slip away. And
had I tried to hold on to it, what would I have achieved? It
would have gone from me in any case. And I would have been
left disconsolate, embittered, convinced that I had been
cheated.

But it is not only the sunlight that must slip away — our
youth goes also, our years, our children, our senses, our lives.
This is the nature of things, an inevitability. And the sooner we

make our peace with it the better. Did I urge myself a moment ago to hold on? I would have done better, it now begins to appear, to have preached the opposite doctrine of letting go — the doctrine of Socrates who called life a *peisithanatos,* a persuader of death, a teacher of the art of relinquishing. It was the doctrine of Goethe who said: *Entsagen sollst du, sollst entsagen,* Thou shalt renounce. And it was the doctrine of the ancient rabbis who despite their love of life said: He who would die, let him hold on to life.

It is a sound doctrine.

First, because, as we have just seen, it makes peace with inevitability. And the inevitable is something with which everyone should be at peace. Second, because nothing can be more grotesque and more undignified than a futile attempt to hold on.

Let us think of the men and women who cannot grow old gracefully because they cling too hard to a youth that is escaping them; of the parents who cannot let their children go free to live their own lives; of the people who in times of general calamity have only themselves in mind.

What is it that drives people to such unseemly conduct, to such flagrant selfishness, except the attitude which I have just commended — a vigorous holding on to life? Besides, are there not times when one ought to hold life cheap, as something to be lightly surrendered? In defense of one's country, for example, in the service of truth, justice, and mercy, in the advancement of mankind?

This, then, is the great truth of human existence. One must not hold life too precious. One must always be prepared to let it go.

And now we are indeed confused. First we learn that life is a privilege — cling to it! Then we are instructed: Thou shalt renounce!

A paradox, and a self-contradiction! But neither the paradox nor the contradiction are of my making. They are a law written into the scheme of things — that a man must hold his existence dear and cheap at the same time.

Is it not, then, an impossible assignment to which destiny has set us? It does not ask of us that we hold life dear at one moment, and cheap at the next, but that we do both simultaneously. Now I can grasp something in my fist or let my hand lie open. I can clasp it to my breast or hold it at arm's length. I can embrace it, enfolding it in my arms, or let my arms hang loose. But how can I be expected to do both at once?

To which the answer is: With your body, of course not. But with your spirit, why not?

Is one not forever doing paradoxical and mutually contradictory things in his soul?

One wears his mind out in study and yet has more mind with which to study. One gives away his heart in love and yet has more heart to give away. One perishes out of pity for a suffering world and is the stronger therefor.

So, too, it is possible at one and the same time to hold on to life and let it go, provided — well, let me put it this way:

We are involved in a tug-of-war: Here on the left is the necessity to renounce life and all it contains. Here on the right, the yearning to affirm it and its experiences. And between these two is a terrible tension, for they pull in opposite directions.

But suppose that here in the center I introduce a third force, one that lifts upward. My two irreconcilables now swing together, both pulling down against the new element. And the harder they pull, the closer together they come.

God is the third element, that new force that resolves the terrible contradiction, the intolerable tension of life.

And for this purpose it does not especially matter how we conceive God. I have been a great zealot for a mature idea of God. I have urged again and again that we think through our theology, not limping along on a child's notion of God as an old man in the sky. But for my immediate purpose, all of this is irrelevant. What is relevant is this: that so soon as a man believes in God, so soon indeed as he wills to believe in Him, the terrible strain is eased; nay, it disappears, and that for two reasons.

In the first place, because a new and higher purpose is introduced into life, the purpose of doing the will of God, to put it in Jewish terms, of performing the *mitzvot*. This now becomes the reason for our existence. We are soldiers whose commander has stationed us at a post. How we like our assignment, whether we feel inclined to cling to it or to let it go, is an irrelevant issue. Our hands are too busy with our duties to be either embracing the world or pushing it away.

That is why it is written: "Make thy will conform to His, then His will be thine, and all things will be as thou desirest."

But that, it might be urged, only evades the problem. By concentrating on duty we forget the conflicting drives within ourselves. The truth is, however, that, given God, the problem is solved not only by evasion but directly; that it is solved, curiously enough, by being made more intense. For, given God, everything becomes more precious, more to be loved and clung to, more embraceable; and yet at the same time easier to give up.

Given God, everything becomes more precious.

That sunshine in Dallas was not a chance effect, a lucky accident. It was an effect created by a great Artist, the master Painter of Eternity. And because it came from God's brush it is more valuable even than I had at first conceived.

And the laughter of children, precious in itself, becomes infinitely more precious because the joy of the cosmos is in it.

And the sweetness of our friends' faces is dearer because these are fragments of an infinite sweetness.

All of life is the more treasurable because a great and Holy Spirit is in it.

And yet, it is easier for me to let go.

For these things are not and never have been mine. They belong to the universe and the God who stands behind it. True, I have been privileged to enjoy them for an hour, but they were always a loan due to be recalled.

And I let go of them the more easily because I know that as parts of the divine economy they will not be lost. The sunset, the bird's song, the baby's smile, the thunder of music, the surge of great poetry, the dreams of the heart, and my own being, dear to me as every man's is to him, all these I can well trust to Him who made them. There is poignancy and regret about giving them up, but no anxiety. When they slip from my hands they will pass to hands better, stronger, and wiser than mine.

This then is the insight which came to me as I stood some months ago in a blaze of sunlight: Life is dear, let us then hold it tight while we yet may; but we must hold it loosely also!

And only with God can we ease the intolerable tension of our existence. For only when He is given, can we hold life at once infinitely precious and yet as a thing lightly to be surrendered. Only because of Him is it made possible for us to clasp the world, but with relaxed hands; to embrace it, but with open arms.

14

CONVERSATION WITH
A DYING MAN

By Hayim Greenberg

I HAVE A VIVID recollection of my last meeting with C. A. Friedland a few months before his death. It was early spring, and I had to be in Cleveland for a few days. As on former occasions, when he was in good health and high-spirited, the hospitable *Het Aleph* (as all his friends called him — by his Hebrew initials) looked me up without delay. He knew that I liked quiet spots out of the city, and he at once took me in his car out of town. I no longer remember the exact spot he drove to — it was an old-fashioned tearoom near a lake.

At first our conversation wandered lamely, and for half an hour at least we engaged in a veiled struggle; I tried to lead the talk away from *the* subject, while he seized on every hint and on the remotest associations to force it back to the paramount theme. At this time Friedland already knew that he was doomed, and also that I was aware of his condition. He now wanted to speak of death — of death in general, and not only of the fate that already beckoned to him so closely. I, on the other hand, followed the conventional pattern in such instance and did everything in my power to steer the conversation toward other subjects, important, less important, or even trivial. As if to spite me the waitress "cooperated" with Friedland, and when I complimented her on the neatness of the place and its fine atmosphere and expressed surprise that nobody else was there, she explained that it was too early in the season for

Clevelanders to come there, and those of the neighborhood were almost all away that day attending a funeral — the local doctor had died, and young and old in the vicinity went to pay him their last respects.

Friedland laughed triumphantly. "You see?" he taunted me. "It's decreed from heaven, and there is nothing you can do about it. Now we have come to *the* subject, and you won't wiggle out of it. Let me tell you what I think. You probably believe that you avoid talking of death out of consideration for me. And you may be right, up to a point. . . . But your reluctance springs even more from pity for yourself. It's only natural, and human. When a relatively healthy person avoids the subject of death, he can retain the illusion that he somehow does not belong to the 'society of diers,' to use one of your own expressions. I suspect that you, my friend, fear death much more than I do, despite the fact that, if I make no mistake, you are very near believing in the immortality of the soul. I know — I am being rude in bringing up this, one of the most intimate matters in a man's life. But tell me the truth: Are *you* afraid of death? Very much afraid? And if you really believe in the immortality of the soul, in a hereafter, in any kind of continuity, why should you fear death? Is my question too brutal? You don't have to answer it. If you find this subject painful, I'm willing to have mercy on you . . . well, then, let's talk about Stalin and Hitler, or Jim Farley, or the city manager of Cleveland, or Kabak's novel about Christ, or, if you wish, even about the difference between the active and the passive *sheva.*"

I laughed involuntarily. "No," I said. "If the alternative is a discussion of Hebrew grammar, I prefer to talk about death."

Friedland slapped my back. "Thanks," he said. "You have good taste, but don't ever say this to our Hebrew school pupils. So, let's talk about death, now that we have overcome our fear — not our fear of death, but our fear of talking about it. So why are you afraid of death itself, assuming that you really believe in the eternity of your 'I'?"

I gave him my answer, but I didn't know myself to what extent my words were earnest, and to what extent they were a game. I said:

"Even if I were profoundly convinced of the existence of a

hereafter, I would still not be ashamed of the fear of death. For true believers this is an entirely different kind of fear. Perhaps the word 'fear' doesn't describe it and another term is needed. In Hebrew we often speak of a state of 'trepidation' which, you know better than I do, is very remote from the concept 'fear'. It is a dread anticipation of a very solemn moment, perhaps the most solemn that the human mind can conceive. One often seeks to postpone also solemn moments, or journeys to unknown though intriguing places. Incidentally, like everyone else I also must have dreaded being born. If I could recreate my emotions a few minutes before I was born, I might 'recall' that I very much did not want to emerge and to transfer my existence from one area to another. Let's not talk about your or my feelings; but as a general rule, what you call 'fear' of death in no way invalidates for believers the genuineness of their belief."

At this point Friedland interrupted me. "I see," he said, "that your knowledge of Freud is coming in very handy. Freud popularized the concept of the birth trauma, or, more correctly, the *conception* that the act of birth must be a shock for the newborn. Let's assume that this is so, but what would Freud say if he were to see you apply one of his scientific concepts in the interests of — I beg your pardon — highly artificial mysticism? This reminds me, by the way, of what Bialik once told about Mendele Mokher Sefarim in his old age. Talking about death, 'Grandpa' used to indulge his fantasy. When a child is born, he would say, his parents and relatives and friends are happy. Congratulations! *Mazel tov!* But it is also possible that in some other world which the little creature left in order to be born here, there is at the same time mourning and weeping. Maybe the same thing happens when one of us dies. We mourn the departed. But who can prove to us that in some remote world into which our departed one was just born, they don't drink toasts, and congratulate each other, and hang charms on the walls to protect the infant from devils and evil spirits? See what kind of nonsense even a stern and disciplined thinker can end up with, if he doesn't make up his mind once and for all that the end is just that, and not a new beginning? . . . But why do you drink your tea so strong? Should I ask the waitress to bring more hot water? And why do you chain-smoke? Medically speaking, you are bringing your new birth nearer, as Mendele would have put it, and I suspect that you are not too anxious to be born again so soon. . . . But I want to ask you something else. I think it was you who once told me about some Russian sect which believed in immortality, which did not admit that death was a natural law. What became of that sect? Now I recall, they believed that only those who do not believe in their own immortality die; all instances of death, from Adam down, were mere 'accidents,' because people did not know the truth. If I remember right, they had empirical proof. Their oldest member was more than two thousand years old, and he was none other than John the Baptist in person, and he used to relate personal recollections about Herod and Jesus. He did not die because he believed in the immortality of his body. (And that fool, Salome, thought she had the head of John the Baptist on her tray.) But one beautiful day, as they say in books, the 'empirical proof' lay down and died, and the sect disintegrated. . . . See what a wonderful memory I have? As Jews say: 'Trivia sticks in the mind.' But perhaps I am unfair to that sect. Why is their theory any more foolish than a dozen others like it? You yourself once told me that this sect consisted of ignorant peasants who somehow sensed that the methods of natural science were the fashion of the day, so when they sought immortality they wanted to find it in terms of flesh and blood instead of in some anemic, otherworldly abstraction. If one is to live forever, then let it be regular life, with eyes and ears, with sunny days and moonlit nights, with color and sound and movement and rhythm, and the warm touch of flesh. . . . It seems to me there is much more sense in the Muslim concept of Paradise with its fountains and flowers and cool sherbet and dancing girls than in the 'Glory of the Godhead' of philosophers and Jewish and Christian religious comforters. It makes more sense because it is at least understandable. But when I listen to the words of all sorts of metaphysical survivalists, it seems to me that they wish to assure me that when, God willing, I will leave my death agonies behind me, I will be consoled with a beautiful gift — the eternity of the geometrical point. Very well, perhaps the geometrical point does exist forever, but if this is the eternity which the Lord of the Universe has in store for me, I am willing to renounce it. I don't know what it means, and it doesn't appeal to me in the least. . . . But here I go — talking too much again, and your tea is getting cold, and you haven't even touched your sandwich; just smoking and smoking. . . . But, come to think of it, if you haven't become a heretic so far, I won't make you one. Nor am I interested in depriving you of your illusions, if you are still capable of clinging to them. If you really believe in a hereafter, I hope you enjoy your belief — in this world. We haven't seen each other for some time, and I feel the need to chat with you, just that. So let's go on. What do you think? Assuming there really is a hereafter, do you think it exists for everyone, or only for spiritual aristocrats, for Chosen Ones? Does every Tom, Dick, and Harry have an eternal existence, or is the hereafter achieved by effort or merit — wisdom, or great scholarship, or sanctity, or perhaps even courage?"

Friedland's question reminded me of a description of the funeral of Emperor Franz Josef which I had read sometime before in an essay by Franz Werfel. The funeral procession halted in the New Market before the monastry of the Capuchin monks, where the members of the Hapsburg dynasty were traditionally interred. The gate of the monastery was locked, as if no one had been expected there on that day. The royal master of ceremonies stepped forward and loudly pounded on the gate with his ornate staff. From within a monk called out: "Who is that, demanding to be admitted?" The master of ceremonies, uniformed and standing at attention, answered loudly and distinctly, stressing each syllable, so that the monk should not misunderstand him: "This is His Royal, Imperial, and Apostolic Majesty, Franz Josef the First, Emperor of Austria, King of Hungary, King of the Lombards and Venetians, King of Bohemia, King of Galicia, King of Croatia and Slovenia, King of Jerusalem, Prince of Silesia, Prince of Bukowina, Prince of Styria, Salzburg, Carinthia, Carniola, and Windshnark, Count of Tyrol, and Ruler over Trieste." The voice of the unseen monk answered briefly and curtly from within: "I know him not." Again the master of ceremonies announced the more condensed and modest title of the deceased, instead of the fully detailed one. But again the monk flung it back with, "I know him not." The third time the master of ceremonies said: "A poor, sinful man seeks admittance," and now the monk replied, "I know him," and opened the gate.

"Here is the answer to your question," I told Friedland. "When the final rest is concerned, the Capuchin monks know neither king nor emperor, nor even one whom the Church considers an apostle; they know only the poor and sinful man, no matter what his status was on earth, and only for him do they open the gate: 'This is the gate . . . wicked men shall enter it.' "

Friedland smiled enthusiastically. The artist in him was aroused. "This is a magnificent tale," he said. "A truly magnificent and touching ritual. I wonder if Shakespeare knew of this custom when he wrote *King Lear*. But — and this is irrelevant to our discussion — isn't it strange that you should draw on Christian religious practices for illustrations? But what would you do if you were talking to an Orthodox Jew? Wouldn't you shock him with your *proof* from Catholic ritual?"

Friedland had been a teacher for many years, and it now seemed to me that he looked at me like a teacher examining a pupil.

"An Orthodox Jew," I answered, "would not ask me such a question. He would know without my telling him that 'All Israel has a share in the world to come' — the genius and the simpleton, the saint and the sinner, Moses and Elisha. An Orthodox Jew might add that some will go directly to paradise while others will go to hell; but aren't both of these hereafter, existence, continuity? The point I tried to make is very simple: There exists no logical or scientific compulsion to accept the idea of immortality. One who feels compelled to believe is subject only to a certain moral compulsion — the impossibility of becoming reconciled to the thought that a sadistic principle underlies the basis of the world, the principle by which creatures are endowed with an urge for immortality and then are slaughtered like sheep. It is therefore impossible for the truly religious to distinguish between 'great' and 'small,' where the immortality of the soul is concerned. Everything is great in its fundamental drives, and everything is small when compared with the Absolute. That is why I feel that Maimonides was guilty of blasphemy (the *real* Maimonides of *The Guide for the Perplexed,* not the political one with his thirteen dogmas including the belief in physical resurrection) when he promised immortality only to human beings who would come into the hereafter in possession of 'active reason,' while those who lived their earthly lives only with their 'natural reason,' or 'passive reason,' he doomed to eternal extinction. Only an intellectual snob could have formulated such an idea, only one who did not realize that his entire 'acquired wisdom' might not be worth a pinch of snuff in the true world of the hereafter. Maimonides (and he was not the first nor the only one among philosophers in this regard) thus libeled God. He profaned what is most important and holiest in man — the essence of humanity, which is infinitely more important than anything one might accumulate round and about this essence. . . ."

For some minutes we were silent. Friedland gazed at the bars of sunlight that stretched from the window to our table. Then, without looking at me, and as if speaking to himself, he said: "This must be true. If there is immortality, it exists for everyone. But to assume immortality also means assuming the existence of God. God alone, were He to exist, could be a guarantee of immortality. But where is God?"

I don't know how this conversation affected Friedland; for me it was too much. I was suddenly afraid, and my skin crawled: How was it possible to sit at a table cluttered with the leftovers of sandwiches and tea and carry on such a conversation with a "candidate" for death who was soon to be called?

Friedland scanned me with a probing glance. "I think" he said, "that you are trying to recall something, a poem perhaps, and your memory doesn't respond."

He was right. I tried to recall some verses from Wordsworth's "Tintern Abbey," and they eluded me. Friedland knew English poetry to perfection and had a phenomenal memory. I told him the opening few words of the fragment I was trying to recall, and he at once recited it in his clear and lyrical voice:

> . . . And I have felt
> A presence that disturbs me with joy
> Of elevated thoughts, a sense sublime

Of something far more deeply interfused
Whose dwelling is the light of setting suns,
And the round ocean and the living air,
A motion and a spirit that impels
All thinking things, all objects of all thoughts
And rolls through all things.

"Was this supposed to be your answer to my question, 'Where is God?' " he said when he had finished. "A very weak answer, my friend, a poetic answer. And what is poetry? What is art? 'A lie in the extramoral sense,' as Nietzsche said. A magnificent, intriguing, perhaps even genial lie, which should be forgiven if only because it distracts the eye to a mirage and prevents it from looking at the abyss of absolute void that awaits all of us. But it is better to know the truth, the brutal, naked, terrible truth that the world is matter — senseless, spiritless, blind, deaf, inanimate matter, and that there exists no 'spirit that impels' either within or above such a world. Since this is so, it is obvious that there can be no immortality in it. It is this truth that one must become accustomed to and cease fearing. All our values — beauty, sanctity, goodness — are our human, subjective values, and they are unknown on other planets because there is no one there to know them. Please do not ask me to explain the incidence of human spirit in a spiritless universe. How should I know? If the existence of human spirit is a miracle, then it is no less a miracle, nor more understandable, than a universe filled with will, knowledge, and above all, conscience. It is terrifying, but I feel it to be the truth, and we have no choice but to take advantage of this 'accident' on one of the least of the planets and to live heroically, and to make the earth as livable as possible, and to cultivate, as long as we live, our sense of truth, justice, beauty, delicacy, and friendliness during the few years that are at our command. That's all we have at our disposal. And after that? There is no 'after that,' and there is no purpose, and we must learn not to fear the *void* that swallows us individually and in groups. . . ."

It was getting late, and we had to return to the city. On the way to the car Friedland concluded: "I don't know exactly when it will happen, but sometime this year I will die. Should you see me in your dreams, I beg you, don't say that I came to *visit* you in a dream. There will be no one to come visiting, and there will be no more *I*. Simply your memory will evoke a remembered image in a dream. I tell you this because I believe that dreams are one of the most important causes for the belief in immortality."

We parted near his car before my hotel. *He* asked forgiveness of *me*: "Perhaps I made you feel sad with my talk. I shouldn't have done it. Now you will be alone in your room with a weight of gloom that I loaded you with. Please excuse me."

"Excuse me" were the last words I heard from him.

PART FOUR

Some Personal Encounters

IN THIS SECTION we bring together not philosophical essays nor historical studies but personal testimonies. They are arranged in a progression from the moment of loss through the experience of burial to the week of *shivah* and then through the year of mourning.

One of the things that emerges from a reading of these testimonies is an awareness of how the Jewish rituals help to move the mourner through the stages from despair to reconciliation. At the moment of loss the overriding emotion is a sense of isolation and of orphanhood, but one of the themes of these testimonies is that as one lives through the year of public observance of grief one develops a sense of ever-widening community. The experience makes us aware that we are all members of "the fraternity of mourners," as one author calls it. Some sooner, some later, all mankind must eventually join this fraternity, and all of us must pay the very same dues. The fraternity is an international one, and so it is possible to say the same prayers and to feel the same sense of kinship, even when traveling in foreign lands, as one of these authors testifies. It is this sense of community, in which the minyan, as the embodiment and the representative of the whole House of Israel, past, present, and future, here and across the world, reaches out and embraces the mourner and takes him into their midst, that mitigates his grief and lessens the sense of orphanhood that death inflicts upon him.

151

15

DEATH BE PROUD

By Michael Braude

I REMEMBER READING a tender and sensitive book by John Gunther that described his reactions to the death of his son. At the time, I was in the fifth grade and the book made a tremendous impression upon me. One impression has changed.

Now, twenty-four years later, I have had occasion to devote a lot of soul-searching to that book. It was entitled *Death Be Not Proud*. Our little boy, Danny, died of a massive virus infection two months before his fourth birthday. As I set my reactions to this on paper I have to title it: *"Death Be Proud."*

I could title it "Death Be Unbearable." Surely today the burden of his loss represents a seemingly unbearable responsibility to his mother and father. The day he was born, his mother and I found Camelot, and his death can be likened to our departure from Camelot. Yet we will bear it, and "unbearable" does not fit.

I could title it "Death Be Harsh." Our first obvious reaction to this abrupt exit from Camelot was precisely, "What can be more harsh or cruel than a child dying in his fourth year?" However, sober thought and reflection reveals that if we have any faith, unless we belong to a Godless cult, and we do not, then we are incapable of deeming any death "harsh."

I could title it "Death Be Sad." Sad it was and is, not only for Danny's parents and little brother but all his relatives and friends and for everyone whose life he touched. However, a

neighbor wrote, "I will always remember Danny as that wonderful, bright, happy little boy who took a walk by our house
with his daddy every day and made our lives a little happier."
That kind of remembering, which I am confident will endure,
cannot be called "sad."

If I eliminate "unbearable," "harsh," and "sad," why do I
contradict Mr. Gunther and turn to "proud?" Because Danny's
death, as well as his life, instilled an important pride in some
significant institutions that are an important part of the process
of living. Moreover, these are institutions that much of contemporary thought tends to attack. What are some of these institutions, and why the pride?

One very *in* thing to do today is to vilify doctors and the
entire medical profession. Danny's death clearly demonstrated
dedication and compassion on the part of doctors to the point
that no patient or patient's family could have asked for more. A
team of our area's best doctors worked three days practically
around the clock to save that little boy. Through it all, they
were candid with his parents but also very tender. When medical science could not prevail, they wept with us and they wept
honest tears. Pride in medicine is what I speak about.

Religion is brushed aside by many people today who say it
has become out of tune with our times. Let any of those people
witness a rabbi missing only his second Friday-night service in
over thirty years to maintain a hospital vigil with distraught
parents. Let any of those scorning know that the rabbi did not
attempt to explain; he only succeeded in comforting. Let any of
those critics realize that when it was over, without a strong faith
in God we absolutely would not have made it. Pride in religion
is what I speak about.

Friendship and the desire to reach out to others is called
passé by many social observers today. We are told that today's
American is cold, heartless, and self-seeking. Precisely the opposite is what this ordeal taught us. A dozen or so close friends
with whom we shared many happy moments stopped their
normal patterns of living for eighty hours and shared and truly
softened our pain while we waited in vain. Neighbors who were
simply people Danny and I waved at as we walked by their
houses every day came forth with sincere, meaningful expres-

sions of sympathy. Even the most casual acquaintances made it a point to convey not only their sorrow but to ask, "How can we help?" Pride in true friendship is what I speak about.

One of those casual acquaintances asked me what might seem to be a strange question under the circumstances; yet I found it provocative and with pride I can forthrightly answer it. He asked, "If before he was born, you could have known that Danny would live such a short time, would you have wanted him to be born?"

Of course we would. Danny's life was three years and nine months of total and complete happiness and joy for us. Obviously this shattering experience teaches a valuable lesson, namely, we must all enjoy and nurture our pleasures while we have them.

Daniel Miller Braude left a rich legacy. That little boy a *Kansas City Star* photographer picked out to photograph at the City Market early this summer lived the way we all want life to be. He was happy, and that infectious smile attracted many people. He was unselfish and in the twenty-one months he was a brother he left our little son, Peter, with the same kind of giving-type personality. He was proud and he left his mother and father with that same pride in life.

Our lives will never be the same, but we too are proud to have had the opportunity to share an all too small portion of them with "that wonderful, bright, happy little boy."

16

MY FATHER "MOVED"

By Max Lerner

MY FATHER DIED on Saturday, as gently and peacefully as he had lived, and he was buried yesterday. At eighty-seven he had lived beyond the biblical assignment, yet even an old man leaves a gaping hole when he breaks through the skein of life and hurtles into no-being.

As I stood at his grave, listening to the service that has come down through the centuries, my mind wound back through the corridors of his life. He came of a line of scholars, men of the Book, simple folk who warmed themselves by the lamps of the past and gloried in the exploits and tragedies of their people.

In Russia he had studied at a yeshivah, and traveled from village to village as an itinerant scholar. But czarist society was stifling. My father and his young wife wanted a chance to earn something and wanted their children to breathe a freer air and become someone. At thirty-three, in 1903, he came to New York as part of the great migration of the century, and my mother followed in 1907 with her four children. He went through the familiar immigrant odyssey: He was a small peddler, worked in a garment loft, became a Hebrew teacher, turned to farming and failed at it, tried a milk-delivery route, became a small grocer. Finally he went back to what he loved — his work as a Hebrew teacher, keeping at it until a few years before his death.

His was one of the millions of American stories that have

woven the history of this country. Life was not easy for my father. He had disappointments, frustrations, tragedies. He was never a big success at anything, nor did he make a great noise in the world. But he loved and was loved, and he had joy in his children. Had he stayed behind in Europe he and they would long ago have been ashes at Auschwitz or ciphers in a Soviet ant-society.

When I saw him toward the end of his illness, while he could still talk, he asked me to bring him his notebooks. They were a confusion of ledgers, journals, loose sheets, on which over the years he had written his reflections on a variety of themes, covering his life within and the world outside, dealing with the early prophets and the latter-day secular figures, with Hitler and Stalin and Nasser, Roosevelt and Truman, Weizmann and Ben-Gurion.

I am, alas, an ignorant man. With all my years of schooling I am unable to read the languages in which my father wrote, as my sons are already able to read mine. I shall save the bundle of pages on which he spent the burden of his hours, driven as he was by a strange necessity to find a garment for what he felt and dreamed.

Someday I may repair my ignorance and discover what thoughts they were that coursed through the mind of this patient, reflective man.

His killer — the killer of so many — was cancer. Mercifully, once it struck it did its work fast. In his last few days he was unconscious.

I think I was the last person whom he saw and recognized. When he whispered my name, I felt a stab of the fitness of it. Surely it is a good thing for a father, in his final moments of consciousness, to know that his son is near him. The father-son relation is the basic link of continuity in life, carrying the male principle and the tradition of responsibility from one generation to the next.

The need for a father is as crucial as the need for a son, and the search of each for the other — through all the days of one's life — exempts no one. Happy the man who finds both.

My father was a gentle and permissive man. When I think of him I think of the lines of the great E. E. Cummings poem:

> My father moved through dooms of love
> Through sames of am through haves of give,
> Singing each morning out of each night
> My father moved through depths of height. . . .
> Because my father lived his soul
> Love is the whole and more than all.

Death seems all the more pitiless when it comes to these gentle people. When I last saw my father, just before he died, he seemed so shrunken and wasted that I fear I broke down shamelessly and wept. It was for more than my father that I wept. It was for death which shows up the final helplessness of life, and for the crazy, tragic absurdity of the whole human condition.

And then, along with the other mourners, I heard and spoke the thunderous syllables of the great Kaddish — *Yitgadal veyitkadash shmeh rabba* — and I looked at the little huddle of my father's friends of many years who stood around, and the absurdity became a little less absurd. Even the most rational of us must admit that there is a healing power in the ritual words when you face what reason cannot fathom.

I keep thinking of my father's last words to me. I had been sitting by his side while he slept. Then my father moved a bit, and his eyes half opened. I bent close to him and barely made out his whispered words. "They are calling from Zion," he said.

It is a good belief with which to die.

17

DEATH IN JERUSALEM

By Jacob Neusner

WHEN THE GREAT TRUMPET sounds and the dead arise from their graves, the shortest walk to the place of assembly will be for the mighty and important, who are buried on the Mount of Olives. But soon they will be joined by those who were buried on *Har Hamenuhot,* the Mount of Rest, on the other side of Jerusalem. From that stark and beautiful hill, with sweeping views in all directions, overlooking the road into Jerusalem from the sea, will come the simple folk. They will not tire themselves in the short walk across town. Not for them the vast distances from the far corners of the Exile, rolling through the caverns and tunnels, just a little Sabbath stroll. They will have a chance to stretch their legs after the rest of the ages.

Among them will be the best friend I ever had, Max Richter, my wife's father and children's grandfather. He died on a sunny morning in Jerusalem, which was never far from his mind. No matter how or where or when, we must accept the judgment: *tzidduk hadin* is especially hard when death is sudden and due to an accident.

Jerusalem's *hevra kaddisha* is deserving of its name, "the holy society." Those beautiful Jews showed me more of what it means to be a Jew, of what Torah stands for, than all the books I ever read. They tended the corpse gently and reverently, yet did not pretend it was other than a corpse. We came to the simple outdoor hall to take up the body. First came *keriah,* making a tear in our garments, performed with proper intent. Then, on a plain leather stretcher, the body was brought forth, wrapped only in shrouds. The *hesped*, eulogy, was the Fifteenth Psalm, which he had loved, and a passage from Ben Sira on wisdom, which he had honored. Then the elder of the *hevra kaddisha* chanted the words of Aquabia ben Mahalalel about from where man comes and where he goes. The voice was sweet, the words solemn. Death is part of life; you cannot have one without the other. You cannot hide from it. But when death comes, you must not curse life.

From there to the resting place, overlooking the main road to Jerusalem. Let no one enter and forget his ultimate destination, even at the threshold of the holy city. The cemetery is kept clean and neat, full of trees, everywhere the sun, purifying and warming.

The body was carried to its final place, let down into the grave with care and thought, yet finality. A few appropriate words, all of them very philosophical, again *Yitgadal veyitkadash*, while earth was being shoveled into the grave, on top of slabs of stone covering the body. From time immemorial this is how Jews buried their dead.

"The holy society" did what Jewish law requires, gently, reverently, and faithful to the law. Here was a stranger and a strange family, from far away. But all was done so kindly and thoughtfully, yet so wholly without sentimentality, that we were able to accept the Judgment and say "amen," as is our duty. The simple words, said slowly and with thought, the measured gestures and the necessary deeds, the careful handling of the corpse, all came to an end with *Yitgadal veyitkadash* and with this apology, in a loud voice, that the dead should hear, and the living, "Mordecai ben Menahem, all that we have done is for your honor. And if we have not done our task properly, we beg your forgiveness."

18

THE MEANING OF THE KADDISH

By Leo Jung

HAVE YOU EVER stood at the open grave of a dear relative? Have you ever felt the dignity, the terror, and the beauty of death? Have you ever heard a wooden voice dead to all emotion, or the voice of a broken heart, of a soul that is crushed — have you heard them say, *"Yitgadal veyitkadash shmeh rabba"*? Have you ever stopped to wonder what these words might mean — whether they are a lamentation for the dead, or if perchance they may bring to you a message from that bourn whence none return?

Have you wondered why the most faithless Jew, he who has driven godliness from his life, who has spurned the Rock of the Ages and the traditions of his race — why even he will find the way back to the synagogue, will appease some secret longing in his heart by mixing with the old-fashioned folk who every day seek contact with their Maker? Do you feel there is some magic in the Kaddish, some mystic formula that will hold the heart, though one fails to grasp its meaning?

What was the life purpose of the Jew who believed in the Kaddish? Why the anxiety of our parents to have a "Kaddish," someone to pronounce those strange Aramaic words when they have joined the ranks of the sleepers?

There is a term in Jewish lore and life which may be called peculiarly Jewish. It is quite unknown outside Jewish spheres of thought, and it fits the peculiar Jewish mentality. It is the phrase *kiddush hashem.* Where a Jew may be weak, because temptation is too alluring, this word will give him strength to resist. Where a Jew may be lacking courage to face a mob of bloodthirsty ruffians in a pogrom-swept land, or on any of the fields which have drunk Jewish blood; where a Jew may hesitate to bring a sacrifice too heavy for the everyday spirit of man, flash that word before his eyes and you will discover heroism and self-sacrifice and strength you would never have divined.

Kiddush hashem means "sanctification of the Divine Name." So close is the affection of the Jew for his God that he dreads doing anything that might offend His dignity, that might in any manner slight the veneration of the great Father of Israel. So ingrained is our love for God that we sink all our small objections and rise to the heights, wherever *kiddush hashem* is at stake.

To live so that our life may be a glory unto God, a source of added devotion among Jew and Gentile, that was the great ambition of true Jews. *Kiddush hashem* was not only the theme of some great occasion, the reaction of the Jew to some soul-stirring event; it was the motto of his life.

It often meant ascending the scaffold on which the tortured Jew breathed his last. It meant, in thousands of cases, weary wandering from shore to shore, going astray in the wilderness of life, with human beasts of prey howling their wild cries into panicky ears. It meant unceasing struggle against efforts to destroy our substance and our honor. It meant facing every terror that fiendish cruelty, that blind hatred could devise, every degradation of bigotry and hypocrisy. It was a white light of godliness among the murky flames of human perversity and inhuman folly.

As the Jew learned the duties of life, this was his greatest goal. As he founded his home, this became his undying light, his *ner tamid.* As he saw his years roll by, this was his greatest concern. As God blessed him with children, with sons to face the turmoil of life, with daughters to kindle a Sabbath lamp not to be dimmed during the week; as he saw the babes develop into boys and girls; as he felt his own powers grow weaker and their energies extend and increase; this was his main care —

that they become bone of his bone, heart of his heart, soul of his soul; that they take upon themselves the glory of his supreme duty to feel personally and continually responsible for the *kiddush hashem* of their days. As he felt his days numbered, his last moments were filled with torture if doubt beset his soul. Will my son remain a Jew, a good Jew? Not one who uses the name as a mere flag, or as an occasional outlet of excessive energy. But will they who have my name, my possessions, my work, my fruits, will they prove strong or weak, true sons of Israel, or mere pursuers after the idols of the multitude?

His last tears were as his first prayers, his last hopes as his first care: "May the Almighty bless my child, that happiness and health be his lot; may He give him joy of life and strength and plenty; but, above all, may He give him eyes to see, a heart to feel where glory lies, where duty is and honor. May He open his heart and strengthen his mind; may He help him and enable him to be and remain a Jew." With this wish he closed his eyes, commending his soul to God.

The father's heart beat no more. The kindly eye was closed forever. No more on this globe were they to meet — son and father. The son had stepped into the parent's shoes. He had undertaken the responsibilities for the honor of his house. And there at the open grave he did not wail and lament. There at the last terrible meeting with his beloved he did not engage in eulogies. There he stood in the presence of the whole congregation of friends and strangers, before those of the age passing and those who were to lead in the age after him, and there at the saddest moment of his life he recalled neither his sorrow nor his loss, but his duty. As as a Jew he knew the holiness of the moment, and he framed his resolution in the words holiest to Jewish hearts; there he opened his lips to Jewish hearts; there he opened his lips and made a pledge, a holy promise: "*Yitgadal veyitkadash shmeh rabba*, Lord God, I do not murmur against Thy decree, I am a child of Jewry. Lord God, hear my voice at this moment. As my father lived for Thee, as his life was dedicated to Thy glory and Thy name, so do I declare *Yitgadal veyitkadash*, 'that Thy great Name may be magnified and sanctified' as the promise for my future. So do I undertake to remember his fidelity, and never to forget my own duty."

That was the meaning of Kaddish in the generations of our fathers. That is the meaning of the words today when said for mother and father. Not a prayer for the dead, but a pledge from the living; not a superstitious phrase, but a man's motto of life.

That is the meaning of *hazkarah* — that we continue where our parents ceased; that we do not allow the heritage of Israel to decay for want of men with the courage to bring sacrifices in a godless, thoughtless world.

Kaddish is the eternal appeal to the divine spark in every Jewish soul. It is the "river of light," the stream of idealism in which the elect bathe for their eternal rejuvenation. From its fire the historical body of our people draws the secret of its eternity. The Kaddish is the living consciousness of our obligation to add Jewish assets to those acquired by the generations before us — to save God for the world. It is the great "Remember!" of the Jew, sounding from the dawn of history, the *kazkarah* which calls out: "Our Father in heaven. We have remembered; we are conscious of Thy grace and our defection. We remember our task and our negligence; the glory of our mission and our deep failings. Do Thou remember, our God! Do Thou make an end to the terror and the grief, the slaughter of the innocent, the terrible night of Thy people!

"Give Thou unto us peace and strength.

"Banish Thou the shadows of the past, and let the glorious light of Thy grace illumine human darkness.

"Yitgadal veyitkadash shmeh rabba" – "Sanctified and magnified be Thy great name."

19

WE DO NOT STAND ALONE

By Morris Adler

IT IS AN EARLY WEEKDAY MORN. A quiet residential street of the dynamic city is still enveloped in a drowsy stillness. Soon life will awake in its silent and comfortable houses, and noisy children, after a hasty breakfast, will leap through doors, schoolward bound. Men can be seen entering one of the houses. Their bearing is marked by reverence and solemnity. Sorrow has recently visited one of the homes on the street, and friends are gathering for the morning service. Within the residence, candles are lit, *tefillin* and *tallit* are quietly donned, and the voice of prayer is heard in the hushed atmosphere.

Long ago a people developed this practice so rich in meaning that neither the passing of centuries nor the roaring life of a metropolitan center has been able to render it obsolete. The friends are no longer individuals come to express sympathy, each in his particular way, with the feeling that the degree of his own friendship with the mourners dictates. They have coalesced into an *edah*, a community. Though this community is small in numbers, it represents in every religious detail the larger *klal yisrael* of which each identified Jew is part. Thus does a community symbolically and actually share in the sorrow of one of its members. The grief of the individual reechoes in the life of the group. No Jew stands alone in his bereavement, while his personal anguish stands as a wall between him and all those upon whose way in life the dark shadow has not fallen. A people closes ranks and encircles its stricken member with the warmth of brotherly sympathy.

The religious service of this little group, representing the larger community, takes place in the home. It is a tribute to the central position of the home. Where a family lives and loves and fashions the most intimate bonds to link persons one to the other, there you have a sanctuary no less than the synagogue. Its holiness is of no lesser kind than that with which the formal house of prayer of the entire community is invested. The poignancy and sanctity of grief are best expressed in the intimate sanctuary of the home. The sanctuary of the home can never be replaced by synagogue or temple, however large or magnificent.

The prayer is concluded. The imperatives of modern living compel the minyan to dissolve once again into its component individuals who hurry through streets, now filled with romping and laughing children and speeding automobiles, to offices, shops, and plants. The mourners remain. They are, however, no longer completely alone. In the atmosphere of their home the prayers linger and bespeak the solace of a tradition and the brotherhood of a community.

20

THE FRATERNITY OF MOURNERS

By Joseph Zashin

RECENTLY I ENTERED into one of the world's oldest fraternities, the mourners' minyan. From time immemorial this institution has persevered in every age and every land in which Jews have found themselves — it ranks ever renewed as the swift hand of Death descends to bereave a household in Israel.

The fraternity functions in the synagogues and temples, meeting twice daily to participate in the traditional services. Belonging means rising early because morning prayer begins promptly at seven fifteen.

There are no rites or ceremonies of induction. You enter the chapel and take your place at one of the benches. The little group knows why you are there. The sorrow which is still sharply etched on your features is familiar to all of them. They know how difficult is your hour of trial. Little is said. A brief murmur and a heartfelt handshake is enough to make you welcome.

The first few days you follow the service in a mechanical, almost uncomprehending way. The *shames* hovers at your elbow ready to be of help — to point out the page, to assist in your inexpert reading of the Kaddish, to show you how to place the *tefillin* on your forehead and how to wind it upon your arm.

There isn't much time for conversation. Morning services chanted at a rapid pace take better than thirty minutes, and on

Monday and Thursday when the reading of the Torah takes place, it takes more. Then the little group breaks up quickly to make its way to its daily occupations.

You soon gain a familiarity with the service. You are no longer the latest initiate. Another mourner has joined, and then another. You know each of the others now, exchanging greetings each day with Charles and Moe and Gabe and Nat and Sam. You have become familiar with the little mannerisms that mark each one. This one bows stiffly from the waist as he intones the Kaddish, that one sways as he recites the Amidah, another one delivers the Alenu with the gusto of a cheerleader's chant, while another punctiliously folds his tallit with loving care.

Why are these men there day after day? One day the rabbi spoke to us about this loyalty which we associate with the passing of a loved one which leads us to undertake this exacting pattern for the next eleven months of our lives. He said that there is nothing else quite like it, quite so universal in its observance, except perhaps the ceremony of the Bar Mitzvah. These two, the mourner's Kaddish, and the Bar Mitzvah, have so profound a place in our religious attitude that Jews who give little if any thought to the rest of the observances of our faith nevertheless observe these two functions with the most steadfast faithfulness.

And thinking about this I came to a realization of why they are similar and why they are significant. In the first instance, for the Bar Mitzvah, the parent leads the young boy to the synagogue. There he undergoes the period of instruction — so incomprehensible — such strange, difficult material to study, to pore over in endless repetition until it is letter-perfect.

You were a mere boy. You never did get to understand what the religious service was all about, what the endless prayers meant. It was so ancient and so remote and so unrelated to what really interested you. It cut into your time for ball games and for playing with your friends. But you had gone through with it because your parents expected it of you. You had to do it so they could be proud of you on your Bar Mitzvah day.

When it was over you left the synagogue at the earliest

opportunity, not to return to it again except on infrequent occasions. There has been the hiatus of the years. How they have flown by! Enough years for you to have been Bar Mitzvah a second and a third time.

Now you have been brought back to the synagogue. Strange, actually brought back by the same parents who brought you to the synagogue the first time. Except that the parents are not there this time to hover over you practicing the chanting, not there to wonder if you are going to do them proud.

But wait. Maybe the parents are there, in spirit, hovering over you as you renew your acquaintance with the ancient letters, repeating them over and over until you develop a facility in uttering them. You are there in the little minyan group because you know that the parents are proud of the son who rises for the Kaddish which sanctifies the Holy Name of God.

Your parents have brought you back to the synagogue for the second time. This time you are no longer the impatient, harried boy you were, but a mature man, tested and tried by the trials of life, brought back to the synagogue for a second time, for a second chance.

What will it mean this time? Will it be another period of incomprehension, of relief when it is over, again a going away?

Or this time, will you seek the meaning of the prayers? Will you follow the cycle of the Torah? Will you catch an understanding of what is implicit in the words? Will you grasp what your forebears have written in the ancient text with their tears and their anguish, with their wisdom and their insight, with their humanity and their humility, with their reverence and their love?

By their going, your parents have brought you back to the synagogue a second time, for a second chance. Will it be different this time?

21

THE MINYAN IS A COMMUNITY

By Eugene J. Lipman

MY GRANDFATHER gave me a pair of *tefillin* when I became a *Bar Mitzvah*. For three years I put them on six mornings a week at home, and I davened. I participated in a minyan in the synagogue only on Sabbath and on festivals.

With each passing year I became more aware of two things about my daily davening: It took less and less time, and whatever good feelings I had had about it when I was thirteen were gone. So I put my *tefillin* away.

I took them out again only when our eldest son began to prepare for his Bar Mitzvah. I taught him how to put on *tefillin,* and I gave him my Bar Mitzvah set. I taught each son in turn, and each received a set of *tefillin*.

I attended a daily minyan when there was a death or when I was present in a synagogue at the right time, but not otherwise. I was content with the various services I conducted and attended.

For months now, I have been going to a traditional minyan most weekday mornings. My reason is the usual one: I'm saying Kaddish. But I do a lot more than say Kaddish during the forty to fifty minutes I spend in a small *bet hamidrash* each morning.

First, I have discovered a new and deeper dimension in the meaning of the word community. Our minyan is a community. There are twelve to twenty of us present on any given morning. Most of us put on *tefillin*. As I do so, I become aware

169

only gradually of the other men, some already seated and quietly davening, others still standing as they competently put on their *tefillin* and say the requisite *berakhot*. I know most of the men by name now. But we do not speak beyond a nod and a good morning, and the presence of the other men is not a distraction to me.

At an unspoken point in time, one of the men goes to the *bima* and begins to chant the morning blessings. I have never quite figured out who decides who will lead the service. If a man has Yahrzeit, everyone seems to know it, and it is assumed he will lead the davening. Otherwise, without any conversation about it, we take turns, all of us who wish to do so. Some mornings two men divide the service, but not always. On Monday and Thursday, on *Rosh Hodesh* and on festivals, if the cantor is present he reads from the Torah. If not, one or another of the men takes over. I am not sure how *aliyot* are apportioned to the required number of men when the cantor is not present. I have not kept a box score but I have the feeling that there is equity in the distribution of honors. I know there is no regard for bank account or status.

We are a quiet minyan. We are a competent minyan. No one has to announce pages. We sit, we stand, we turn pages, we sing parts of the service together, other parts we sing quietly, each to his own *nigun*. As we daven, we *shokel* each in his own pattern of body-swaying; some stand still. Our variety of Hebrew pronunciations goes from broad *Pailish* to clipped *Sefaradit,* with stops along the way at every major Central and East European center of Jewish life. Rhythm is the hallmark of this communal coming-together — a rhythm of words, a rhythm of body movements, a rhythm of feeling. In some inexplicable way, individuals do their thing; yet the group feeling is intense.

Our minyan is not in a hurry. If I get caught up in a passage or a phrase or a word and I stop to think for half a minute, the minyan hasn't ripped off twenty pages during that time. We start on time, and we end within five minutes of forty minutes later — slow leader, fast leader, it makes little difference. Add five minutes for Torah reading. When we have to say Hallel and Musaf we start ten minutes earlier by prior agreement. No one should ever feel pressed for time.

So at our minyan there is no sense of being rushed. As a result, I have learned a lot about the meanings of many words, phrases, Psalms, passages in the Siddur. I am not alone in expanding my comprehension of the content of the service. From time to time, after services one of the men will comment on something which occurred to him for the first time as he was davening. We all listen whether or not we've known the "new" insight for years. Questions are asked. There are no *klotzkashes*; every question rates a respectful answer, or several answers.

We have a private caterer at our minyan. Charlie voluntarily sets out coffee and cake every morning. Sometimes there's a leftover, something from *Shabbat,* some special rolls someone has brought, a *mandelbrot* baked by someone else's wife. There's always a bottle of schnapps, too, but the "*lehayyim*-drinkers" are few at that time of morning. Mostly it's a cup of coffee, some *schmooz,* "have a good day," perhaps some coins into the *pushke* on the wall — and our minyan's members go out into the world to do its work.

In a normal weekday morning service, there are four opportunities to say the Kaddish. Not once have I felt casual about those moments — not within myself, and not in the feelings coming from the other men, both those saying Kaddish and those sitting and answering "Amen." We say the words quietly. I am completely absorbed in forcing once again to reality and acceptance the fact of my own loss. Yet I hear the other voices. I need to hear them. They support me. They add to my reality for standing and saying those words. I feel for my neighbors, too, and they feel for me. I know it deeply as I stand there.

Once in a while there is jarring note. A man wants to go faster than the rest of us. Without thinking, even without consciousness of what we are doing, the rest of us say the words a bit louder. Within a phrase or two the message has been received and we are in rhythm again, to the last amen.

Occasionally, before it is time to say Kaddish, or after the first Kaddish of the service, a scene may pop into my mind — my forefathers in Yavneh saying that Kaddish d'Rabbanan after a Sanhedrin debate about a matter of *halakhah* we now take for granted; the different accents of Jews in Yemen — or in Kai-Feng-fu — saying the same words; the anxiety in the voices of a minyan in the cellar of a Spanish home in the fourteenth century; my grandfather's minyan in Bialystok when he said Kaddish for his parents; the last minyan in Theresienstadt before we left it forever; the little *shtibl* in Jerusalem where I heard the most fervent Kaddish and said my amen with rare feeling. At those moments, like many Jews, I remember not only for myself and the bitter fact which brings me to the minyan each morning, but I remember for all Jews in all places at all times.

The last Kaddish is said, the *tefillin* and the *tallit* are removed. And in ways I cannot explain, as the effect of causes I do not comprehend, I am ready for my day. I am ready to do what I must do. I am ready to laugh and to enjoy and to fulfill. I am ready for the inevitable reminders of our son's life and death.

Could I be ready without the minyan? I do not know and I do not intend to try to find out. For I do know that those forty to forty-five minutes transform me each day I attend. They clear the way to a day of life.

22

KADDISH IN MANY PLACES

By Seymour J. Cohen

THURSDAY WAS A LANDMARK DATE for me. It was the fifteenth
day of Shebat, an easy day to remember, for it was the new
year of the trees. Yesterday was the first day in eleven months
that I was not required to recite the Kaddish — to join the row
of mourners in remembering their sacred dead. Yesterday was
the beginning of a new year in Israel and of a new stage in my
life. In Israel little saplings were planted on this day. They will
grow into beautiful trees, gracing the landscape of our Holy
Land. In my life many memories were planted during this year
that has now ended. Let me name some of them:

At times during this year I have said Kaddish in some most
unusual places. A few weeks ago, waiting for the plane to Israel
in the El Al terminal, I noticed a family in the corner of the
waiting room who were quite bereft, and whose garments had
been torn with the traditional *keriah*. I was asked, "Would you
like to *daven* Minhah with us?" I joined them in Minhah, and
then, after the service, I asked discreetly about the family. I
learned that they were to fly on the same plane. They were like
the family of our ancestors, Jacob and Joseph, who pleaded
that they not be buried in Egypt, but that their remains be
brought back to the land of their birth. They were bringing
back the remains of a member of their family, born somewhere
in Europe, but in the spiritual sense, born in the land of Israel
three thousand years ago.

On the plane, we had another minyan in the morning. The sun was rising over the Mediterranean, or perhaps we were over the Italian peninsula, and we read from a small Torah scroll that was going to be presented by some congregation to Zahal, the Israeli defense forces. We had no table, so the Torah was held up by two men. A Bar Mitzvah boy read from the scroll, "*Bo el Pharaoh*" — "Go to Pharaoh and tell him to let my people go." I was deeply touched by this. The Bar Mitzvah boy's grandfather had been my teacher in high-school days and taught me Talmud years ago. It was so symbolic. In the hold of the plane were the remains of a Jew who had passed on, and above, in the passenger compartment, a vibrant dynamic minyan was reaffirming its continuity and its faith in God.

During the course of this last year I recited Kaddish many times in our own synagogue chapel. Day after day the minyan starts while it is still pitch-dark. It is an experience to come to this *bet hamidrash* and see how a handful of men make up this daily service and keep up the continuum of praise to God. The individual members of the minyan come and go but the minyan continues every single day of the year, every single year of the synagogue's life. It is touching to see how the members encourage each other, how their friendships develop, how concerned they become if one does not show up for a few days. They are truly a *havurah*, a fellowship, and they care for their *haverim*. In recent weeks, a fine woman has joined the minyan. She comes to pray for the well-being of her grown family and to recall the sacred memory of her mother. At first she seemed an outsider; now she is a part of the group.

During the course of the year I recited Kaddish at the *Kotel Maravi*, the Western Wall. There the tears of Israel have been shed since the destruction of the Temple. I felt privileged saying the ancient words there, and I felt that in a sense I was saying them there as my father's representative, since he never had the privilege of being there.

But there were jollier settings in which I said the Kaddish. There was the Hasidic *shtiblach* to which I had been introduced by my friend, Rabbi Abraham Karp. I had been to Meah Shearim many, many times, but I never knew that just a few yards away from the din of the Meah Shearim marketplace there was another din, not of peddlers and housewives debating the price of fish, but of men raising their voices in prayer. I had been to Jerusalem many times. I didn't know about this particular little set of miniature synagogues, these little spiritual diamonds in the rough. What a charming atmosphere pervades them. "Minhah, Minhah, Minhah," was the cry as I walked in, "we need a tenth man for the minyan." I needed them for my Kaddish, and they needed me for their minyan and so we felt connected, these Hasidim and I, even though we had never met before. The service was the service of the Sephardic ritual. I noticed that the prayer books that they used were very, very torn. My book dealer, Mr. Schreiber, was there, and so I said, "Perhaps you ought to get them some new prayer books. Order them for the synagogue, will you please, and inscribe my father's name." I had never been there before, and I do not know when or whether I will be back there again, but meantime something of me and something of my father's memory is there in those books.

Once a week, on Thursdays, the eve of the eve of the Sabbath, the little people of Jerusalem, the humble beggars, come in to that synagogue. With great dignity they receive their offerings. I noticed one beggar giving a bit of charity to another. This is the custom among these people—even the poorest of men has to help others.

One day, after leaving the "Minhah, Minhah, Minhah" setting, I saw people running. They were loading on lorries, small trucks. "Where are you going?" I asked.

"Why it's the Yahrzeit of the Or Hahayim," the answer came. The Or Hahayim is the famous mystical commentator on the Bible whose works are beloved and revered by both the Ashkenazic and Sephardic Jewish communities. (I once met a cab driver in Jerusalem who goes up to the grave of the Or Hahayim every morning at 4:00 A.M. to light an oil lamp at the grave of this great sage.) The old Yiddish expression has it that if the whole world runs you should run too, so I went to my Hertz car and followed them up to the Mount of Olives. There in one of the oldest burial grounds of Jewish history I came to the grave of the Or Hahayim, where I found the Jews of my little synagogue praying and reciting the words of the Psalms.

In one corner there was a Minhah service. A little while later, as twilight came to Jerusalem, which is a glorious experience in itself, as the blue skies turned gradually to purple and finally to black, there was an Ashkenazic service. For the first time in my life I did not worship in an easterly direction, toward Jerusalem, but instead I prayed toward the west, for the Mount of Olives is east of the Temple site. There I could see the massive walls of Herodian stone that have stood as silent witnesses for thousands of years, testifying to the love of the Jewish people for the city of Jerusalem. I was praying for the first time in a westerly direction, for I was on the other side of the wall, but I could see the Jews at the wall in mind from where I stood, and in my mind I could join my prayers to theirs.

On the way home from Jerusalem last summer, I stopped off in London. One morning I went to a small synagogue near my hotel for services and for Kaddish. I noticed that the leader of the service prayed with the tallit draped over his head. The voice sounded vaguely familiar, but it was not until the service was over and he doffed his tallit and turned around that I realized who it was. It was the Chief Rabbi of England, in mourning for his mother, who was leading us that day in the Kaddish. But until the service was over and he turned around I did not know that. It could have been any ordinary Jew leading the prayers or mourning for his parent. The words were the same and the service was the same and the grief was the same no matter who happened to be leading the prayers.

Yes, there were many, many places and many occasions when I said Kaddish during these eleven months. Of all of them, however, this is the one that means the most to me. A week ago I visited the soldiers at Hadassah Hospital. Those who are still there are the ones who are most difficult to treat. They have been there since the Yom Kippur War, and as I went from bed to bed shaking hands and mumbling a few inadequate words of encouragement to them I felt so feeble, so helpless, so unable to say what I wanted to to them. Finally, after I had spent some time with them, I broke away from the group and went to the synagogue of the hospital to get some emotional relief. I went in there and sat down to look at the

Chagall windows that are so lovely and to be by myself for a few minutes just to think. As I sat studying the windows, I noticed a *mohel*, a circumcisor, come in. I asked him, "When will the Brith be?" "In a little while," he replied. Then a modest Sephardic family and their guests came in. Soon they were joined by the proud father, who was one of the soldiers from the ward upstairs, still in his bandages and still in his cast. Then they brought the little child in, and the Brith began.

At the end of the service, they recited the Kaddish. I don't know for whom but I was delighted to join their quorum. As I did, I sensed the whole cycle of life revolving before me. I had said the Kaddish once on a plane carrying a man to his last resting place. Now I was saying it again as a new life entered the Covenant of Abraham. I was reciting Kaddish for my father, surrounded by the majestic beauty of the Chagall windows, but more than the creation by man was the creation of God. I was thinking of my father, who lay many thousands of miles away, but I was in the company of new kinsmen with whose path mine had now crossed. Somehow, I had the feeling that there is a wondrous continuity, a never-ending flow of life, to death and through death, and that therefore, despite all its aches and all its pains, there is great beauty and great meaning in our lives.

I have said Kaddish in many places and with many different people during these eleven months. The Kaddish has brought me into contact with many Jews, and with my father, and with myself. I think that he would be pleased.

EPILOGUE

To Life!

THIS BOOK'S LAST WORD is a modern ethical will. Because of its intimate nature we have omitted the author's name, but he was a prominent leader of Jewish life, an important businessman and scientist, and a very dear and precious friend. This will was written when he was still in good health and was put away to be opened by his family after his death, which occurred nearly ten years later.

It is an appropriate ending for this book because it brings us back from contemplating death to appreciating life. The last word of a Jewish book on death has to be addressed to life, for we do not study death in order to become morbid or depressed but in order to learn from facing death something about how to live.

In a sense this will by a contemporary Jew brings us back full circle to where we began, to the deathbed descriptions of the Hasidim in the premodern world. Both there and here we are in the company of human beings who departed this life as models, as guides, and as teachers to those whom they left behind. Both there and here the stress is on continuity. Both there and here the last word is to life.

This will is an extraordinary document because of the gentle way in which its author prepares to accept death whenever it may come, because of the concern and guidance that he offers to his loved ones, and because of the simple grace and eloquence with which he summarizes the truths by which he has tried to live and the values that he wishes to convey to those who will come after him. Although it was written for his own immediate family, it contains insights that will speak to the hearts of many others. We are therefore very grateful to his wife and children for giving us the privilege of sharing their document. It is indeed a reflection on death and a prescription for life.

23

TO MY WIFE AND CHILDREN

By W. L. A.

Jerusalem, 1963

Dearest . . . . . ,

Weep not and dry your tears. At least in my behalf. The years that God has allotted to me have been good, and I have no *tayneh* to our Maker. Death is the final state of all human beings, and a few years more or less do not matter. I have drunk fully of the cup of life, and a few remaining drops left unsipped need cause no grief or regrets. If there is one thing I do ask, it is that I may be permitted to see all my children happily married; if not, I'll be watching from somewhere anyway. Marriage is the fulfillment of life, and I have been blessed with a jewel of a wife and four wonderful children whose love has sustained me during those times that try a man's soul and has nourished me during times of *simhah*.

To my wife — Your love has been to me beyond measure. Remember what has been and weep not. Time is a wondrous healer even as you and I have forgotten not our son nor our parents. You are too much a woman to live alone, and the children will mature and go their own way. Look for a man you can respect and love and know that I want only that you be happy.

To my children – In material things I have seen to it that you will not want. These are the least important things, although the lawyer has prepared a megillah to safeguard them. Remember to be Jews, and the rest will follow as day follows night. Our religion is not ritual but a way of life. To us as Jews, life is its own *raison d'être,* its own self-justification; we await neither heaven nor hell. Ritual is only a tool to remind us who we are and of the divine commandments. Jews do not lie, steal, nor bear false witness — *past nisht,* as our parents used to say — such things are simply unbecoming for a Jew. Take care of one another, and in honoring your mother, honor yourselves. I know the love she has lavished on you without thought of self.

Marry within your faith. Not to please me but so that you may be happy. Not because Gentiles are inferior —they are not —but because marriage is complex enough without the complicating variables of different viewpoints. You are the bearers of a proud tradition of four thousand years. Do not let the torch drop in your generation.

Turn not away anyone who comes to you for help. We Jews have seen more suffering than any other people. That which you give away, whether of money or of yourselves, is your only permanent possession.

To my son — I mention you first, not because I love you more, but because you will now be the head of the family. The girls may call this sexism but I hope they will forgive me. Fail not your sisters and your mother. Their tears are my tears. Money is only a tool and not an end in itself. Your grandfather taught me that a man should earn his money until the age of forty, he should enjoy it between forty and fifty, and after fifty he should give it away. A man who dies rich is a failure as a human being. I say this because I know that your abilities will make you a wealthy man materially. But my real desire is that you be rich in heart and soul. Our militant leftist youth have not read their histories. All leftist revolutions have in the end devoured their Jewish initiators. I still remember how my friends at college proclaimed that the victory of the proletariat would end all anti-Semitism in Russia.

Forget not Israel. You can be a builder of the homeland for the remnants of our people. There is no conflict between your obligation as a citizen of our country and your concern for Israel. Your duties to your community and to America need

not suffer beca... rary, a good Jew
is a better citize...

To my daughters — You are warm-blooded. Jewish girls keep themselves clean, not because sex is dirty but because the love you will bring your husbands should not be sullied by experimentation or dalliance. It has always been the Jewish mother who has preserved our people. I shall be content if you follow in the path of your mother.

To all of you — Let your word be your bond. Those mistakes that I regret most keenly are the times when I let human weaknesses forget this. Unfortunately, it is always difficult to learn from the experiences of others, particularly of parents. But if there is one thing I beg you to take to heart, it is this.

Say Kaddish *after* me but not *for* me. Kaddish is the unique Jewish link that binds the generations of Israel. The grave hears not the Kaddish, but the speaker does, and the words will echo in your heart. The only immortality I seek is that my children and my children's children be good Jews, and thereby good people.

God bless you all and keep you.

THE CONTRIBUTORS

Morris Adler (1906–1966) was rabbi of Congregation Shaarey Zedeck in Southfield, Michigan, and the author of many books.

Michael Braude is a member of Congregation B'nai Yehudah in Kansas City, Missouri, and an officer of the Bank and Commerce Trust Company of that city.

Seymour J. Cohen is rabbi of Anshe Emet Synagogue, Chicago, and past president of the Synagogue Council of America. He has edited and translated several works of medieval Jewish ethics and written *A Time to Speak*.

Chaim N. Denburg is a rabbi in Montreal, Canada, and is the translator of the Shulhan Aruk, Yoreh Deah.

Samuel H. Dresner is rabbi of Beth El of Highland Park, Illinois, and the author of *The Zaddik*.

Emanuel Feldman is rabbi of Beth Jacob Synagogue of Atlanta, Georgia, and author of *The 28th of Iyar*.

Audrey Gordon is the director of Beth Emet Synagogue's High School Department in Evanston, Illinois. She has served as assistant to Dr. Elisabeth Kubler-Ross and has taught at Northwestern University and Beloit College.

Hayim Greenberg (1900–1953) was editor of *The Jewish Frontier* and *Der Yiddishe Kempfer* and the head of the Department of Education of the Jewish Agency. His essays were published posthumously in *The Inner Eye*.

Abraham J. Heschel (1907–1972) was professor of Jewish ethics and mysticism at the Jewish Theological Seminary and was the author of nearly two dozen books, including *Man's Quest for God, God in Search of Man,* and *The Prophets*.

Leo Jung is the rabbi of the Jewish Center Synagogue of New York and the author and editor of *Fallen Angels, The Jewish Library* and many other works of Jewish thought.

Abraham Kaplan is professor of philosophy and dean of the Faculty of Social Sciences at the University of Haifa. He is the author of *Love and Death: Talks on Contemporary and Perennial Themes* and other works.

Dr. Elisabeth Kubler-Ross is the author of *On Death and Dying* and has conducted numerous seminars on this theme in hospitals, universities, and elsewhere.

Max Lerner is professor emeritus of American civilization at Brandeis University and columnist for the *New York Post.* He is the author of *America As a Civilization* and other works.

Eugene J. Lipman is the rabbi of Temple Sinai of Washington, D. C. He is the editor of *The Mishnah: Oral Traditions of Judaism.* He is lecturer in Judaism at the School of Sacred Theology of the Catholic University of America.

Deborah Lipstadt is Assistant Professor of History and Comparative Religion and Assistant Chairman of Jewish Studies, University of Washington, Seattle, Washington.

Hans J. Morgenthau is distinguished university professor of government at the City University of New York and the author of many studies in foreign policy.

Jacob Neusner is professor of Jewish history at Brown University and the author of many studies in Talmudic history and Jewish thought.

Jack Riemer is the rabbi of Beth Abraham Synagogue of Dayton and teaches Jewish thought at the University of Dayton. He is the coeditor of *New Prayers for the High Holidays* and author of numerous essays and reviews in Jewish and general journals both here and abroad.

Daniel Jeremy Silver is rabbi of The Temple of Cleveland, Ohio, and professor of religion at Case-Western Reserve University. He is the author of *A History of Judaism* and *Maimonidean Criticism and the Maimonidean Controversy.*

Joseph B. Soloveitchik is a member of the faculty of Yeshiva University of New York and the founder of the Maimonides School of Boston. He is the author of *The Lonely Man of Faith, The Man of Halachah,* and many other studies.

Milton Steinberg (1904-1950) was Rabbi of the Park Avenue Synagogue, and the author of *Basic Judaism, As a Driven Leaf,* and other books.

Elie Wiesel is distinguished university professor in the Department of Jewish Studies at the City University of New York. He is the author of *Night, Dawn, The Town Beyond the Wall, The Jews of Silence, Souls on Fire,* and other novels that have won international acclaim.

Joseph Zashin is a former member of Temple Israel of Great Neck, Long Island. He now resides in Arizona.